CROCHET
BABY SETS

CROCHET BABY SETS

KRISTI SIMPSON

STACKPOLE BOOKS

Essex, Connecticut
Blue Ridge Summit, Pennsylvania

STACKPOLE BOOKS

An imprint of Globe Pequot, the trade division of
The Rowman & Littlefield Publishing Group, Inc.
4501 Forbes Blvd., Ste. 200
Lanham, MD 20706
www.rowman.com

Distributed by NATIONAL BOOK NETWORK
800-462-6420

British Library Cataloguing in Publication Information available

Library of Congress Cataloging-in-Publication Data

Names: Simpson, Kristi, author.
Title: Crochet baby sets / Kristi Simpson.
Description: First edition. | Lanham, MD : The Rowman & Littlefield Publishing
   Group, Inc., [2024]
Identifiers: LCCN 2023030312 (print) | LCCN 2023030313 (ebook) | ISBN
   9780811772600 (paperback) | ISBN 9780811772617 (ebook)
Subjects: LCSH: Crocheting—Patterns. | Infants' clothing.
Classification: LCC TT820 .S52733 2024 (print) | LCC TT820 (ebook) | DDC
   746.43/4041—dc23/eng/20230724
LC record available at https://lccn.loc.gov/2023030312
LC ebook record available at https://lccn.loc.gov/2023030313

♾️™ The paper used in this publication meets the minimum requirements of
American National Standard for Information Sciences—Permanence of Paper for
Printed Library Materials, ANSI/NISO Z39.48-1992.

First Edition

CONTENTS

PATTERNS

Theo Set: Socks, Hat, Vest 44

Molly Set: Onesie, Shorts, Bib 52

Ari Set: Hat, Booties, Blanket 60

INTRODUCTION

The designs in this book will delight maker, mom, and baby! With a wide selection and variety of baby fashion and accessories for newborns to twelve months, these patterns are thoughtfully designed for both baby comfort and crocheting fun. Every pattern set is made with DK-weight yarn and purposefully designed for mixing and matching.

For those who are hesitant, clothing does not have to be intimidating to crochet. It's actually very easy! I have even designed a few pieces that do not include seaming, so you can test your crochet skills. And when it comes to stitching the pieces together, take your time. You'll find that sewing for baby clothes is minimal and it will work out just fine. Baby clothes are fun to make, and you'll find yourself crocheting them over and over!

The patterns are coordinated in groups of threes, but you can mix and match from any set to make your own layette. They can, of course, also be made as individual pieces when one piece is all you need.

I hope that you and baby both enjoy this book!

Best stitches,
Kristi Simpson

TIPS FOR CROCHETING BABY CLOTHING

When you crochet clothing, consider the following tips:

- **Always crochet a swatch with your yarn and the recommended hook size in the pattern to check the gauge.** Check your stitch and row count and get as close as possible to the pattern gauge, not the yarn-label gauge. I once had a lady compare her gauge swatch to the label gauge and her hat was tiny compared to the pattern gauge because the gauges were different . . . so, check before you begin the pattern!
- **Learn the magic ring (sometimes called a magic circle).** It allows you to pull the beginning round tightly so that there isn't a hole in your work. I have also added it to the Stitch Guide (page 94) so you can see step-by-step, how-to instructions to complete this technique. This technique is helpful for hats, socks, flowers, and other items that are worked in rounds.
- **When joining the final round, use the "invisible join" technique.** This technique prevents the knot-like appearance that can result from the "slip-stitch join" technique and allows the final stitch to look like another stitch. It's easy, and directions can be found in your Stitch Guide (page 111).
- **When decreasing, use the "invisible sc2tog" technique.** Instructions are in the Stitch Guide (page 105). You'll love how smooth it looks compared to the traditional sc2tog technique.
- **Count your stitches.** In most of the patterns, rows and rounds vary in counts, so keep track! COUNT! It will save you time, I promise!
- **Use stitch markers.** Keep a stash for marking rows that are mentioned within the pattern or even just to mark the right side of the work, also known as the public side. They help in many different ways other than just marking your starting stitch.
- **When sewing your pieces together, use stitch markers to hold the item in place.** You can also pin the pieces together with extra yarn needles to hold the pieces flat.
- **When seaming pieces together, I use the whipstitch most often.** Place the pieces right sides together so that you are seaming on the "inside" of the finished piece. This piecing technique makes the seam look pretty on the "outside." When you're finished, flip the piece right-side out, and voilà!

PATTERNS

ARLO
SET

BLANKET, HAT, BOOTIES

This crochet set covers all the basics. It includes a blanket, hat, and booties for the baby and only uses a few stitches and a couple skeins of yarn. The stitches are fun and easy and make the finished products look interesting while keeping them fresh and modern. You'll enjoy making (and gifting) this set!

BLANKET

Yarn

Premier Yarns Anti-Pilling Everyday DK; light weight #3; 100% anti-pilling acrylic; 3.5 oz (100 g) / 273 yd (250 m) per ball:

- A: 1070-65 Lake, 3 balls
- B: 1070-19 Linen, 3 balls
- C: 1070-60 Salmon, 3 balls

Hook and Other Materials

- US size H-8 (5 mm) crochet hook
- Yarn needle

Finished Measurements

Width: 28 in (71.2 cm)
Length: 48 in (122 cm)

Gauge

15 dc x 8 rows = 4 in (10.2 cm)

Color Sequence:

Work 2 rows each in A, B, and C, repeating Color Sequence for the length of the blanket.

INSTRUCTIONS

With A, ch 117.

Row 1: Dc in 4th ch from hook, dc in next 2 chs, *sk next 2 chs, dc in next ch, ch 3, 3 fpdc around dc just worked (see Stitch Guide, page 108), sk next 2 chs, dc in next 3 chs; rep from * across, turn.

Row 2: Ch 3 (this stitch counts as a double crochet here and throughout), dc in next 2 dc, *ch 2, sc in next ch-3 sp, ch 2, dc in next 3 dc; rep from * across, turn. Fasten off. Join with color B.

Row 3: Ch 3, dc in next 2 dc, *sk next ch-2 sp, dc in next sc, ch 3, 3 fpdc around dc just worked, sk next ch-2 sp, dc in next 3 dc; rep from * across, turn.

Rep Rows 2 and 3 following Color Sequence until blanket measures 48 in (121.92 cm); end on Row 2.

Fasten off. Join with color A.

Border

Rnd 1: With A, ch 1, 3 sc in first st, sc evenly across each st and in each ch-sp, 3 sc in last st; work sc evenly spaced down side edge; working along opposite side of foundation ch, work 3 sc in ch at base of first sc of Row 1, sc in each ch across to ch at base of last sc, 3 sc in last ch; work sc evenly spaced up next side edge; join with sl st in first sc.

Fasten off. Weave in ends.

HAT

Yarn
Premier Yarns Anti-Pilling Everyday DK;
   light weight #3; 100% anti-pilling acrylic;
   3.5 oz (100 g) / 273 yd (250 m) per ball:
- A: 1070-65 Lake, 1 ball
- B: 1070-19 Linen, 1 ball
- C: 1070-60 Salmon, 1 ball

Hook and Other Materials
- US size G-6 (4 mm) crochet hook
- Yarn needle

Finished Measurements
Newborn (3–6 Months, 9–12 Months)
Circumference: 14 (16, 18) in / 35.7 (40.8,
   45.8) cm
Height: 5 (5¾, 6½) in / 12.8 (14.7, 16.6) cm

Gauge
16 dc x 12 rows = 4 in (10.2 cm)

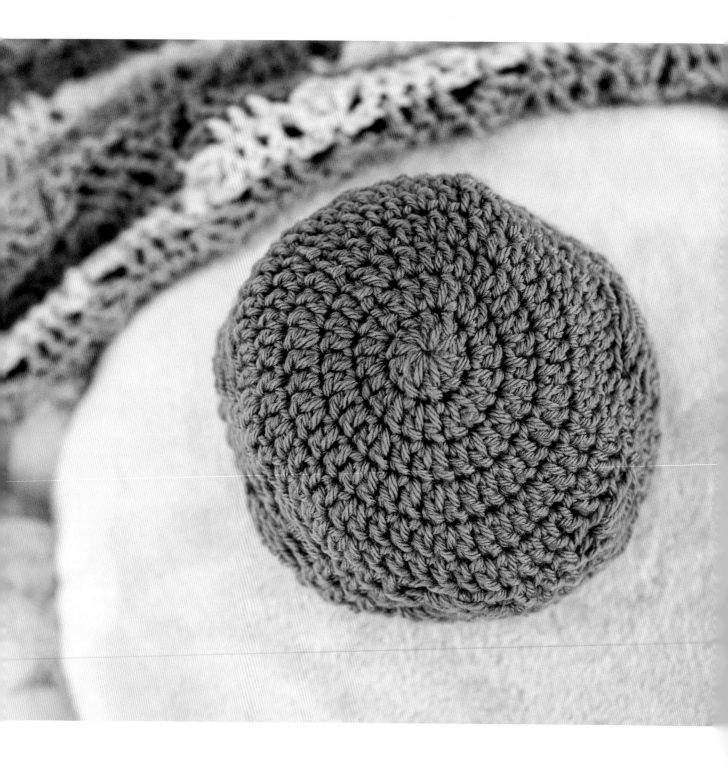

INSTRUCTIONS

With A, create a magic ring (see Stitch Guide, page 94).

Rnd 1: Ch 3 (this counts as a double crochet here and throughout), 9 dc in magic ring, join with sl st to first dc. (10 dc)

Rnd 2: Ch 3, dc in same st, 2 dc in each st around, join with sl st to 3rd ch of beg ch 3. (20 dc)

Rnd 3: Ch 3, 2 dc in next st, *dc in next st, 2 dc in next st; rep from * around, join with sl st to 3rd ch of beg ch 3. (30 dc)

Rnd 4: Ch 3, dc in next st, 2 dc in next st, *dc in next 2 sts, 2 dc in next st; rep from * around, join with sl st to 3rd ch of beg ch 3. (40 dc)

Rnd 5: Ch 3, dc in next 2 sts, 2 dc in next st, *dc in next 3 sts, 2 dc in next st; rep from * around, join with sl st to 3rd ch of beg ch 3. (50 dc)

Newborn only:

Rnd 6: Ch 3, dc in next st, *dc in next 11 sts, 2 dc in next st; rep from * around, join with sl st to 3rd ch of beg ch-3. (54 dc)

Size 3–6 Months only:

Rnd 6: Ch 3, dc in next 7 sts, *2 dc in next st, dc in next 6 sts; rep from * around, join with sl st to 3rd ch of beg ch-3. (56 dc)

6–9 months only:

Rnd 6: Ch 3, dc in next 2 sts, *dc in next 4 sts, 2 dc in next st; rep from * around, join with sl st to 3rd ch of beg ch-3. (63 dc)

All sizes:

Rnd 7: Ch 3, dc in next 2 sts, *sk next 2 sts, dc in next st, ch 3, 3 dc around front post of dc just worked (see Stitch Guide, page 108), sk next 2 sts**, dc in next 3 sts, rep from * around, ending last rep at **, join with sl st to 3rd ch of beg ch 3.

Rnd 8: Ch 3, dc in next 2 sts, *ch 2, sc in next ch-3 sp, ch 2, sk next 3 fpdc**, dc in next 3 dc; rep from * around, ending last rep at **, join with sl st to 3rd ch of beg ch 3.

Rnd 9: Ch 3, dc in next 2 sts, *sk next ch-2 sp, dc in next st, ch 3, 3 dc around front post of dc just worked, sk next ch-2 sp**, dc in next 3 sts; rep from * around, ending last rep at **, join with sl st to 3rd ch of beg ch-3.

Rep Rnds 8 and 9 until hat measures 4¾ (5½, 6¼) in / 12.2 (14, 16) cm; ending on Rnd 8. Fasten off. Join with color B.

Next rnd: Ch 1, sc in each st and ch-2 and ch-3 sp around, join with sl st to first sc made at beg of rnd. Fasten off B. Join with color C.

Last rnd: Ch 1, sc in each st around, join with sl st to first sc made at beg of rnd.

Fasten off. Weave in ends.

BOOTIES

Yarn

Premier Yarns Anti-Pilling Everyday DK; light weight #3; 100% anti-pilling acrylic; 3.5 oz (100 g) / 273 yd (250 m) per ball:

- A: 1070-65 Lake, 1 ball
- B: 1070-19 Linen, 1 ball
- C: 1070-60 Salmon, 1 ball

Hook and Other Materials

- US size G-6 (4 mm) crochet hook
- Yarn needle

Finished Measurements

3–6 Months (9–12 Months)
Width: 2 (2) in / 5 (5) cm
Height: 3 (3½) in / 7.7 (9) cm

Gauge

20 sc x 20 rows = 4 in (10.2 cm)

INSTRUCTIONS

Size 3-6 Months:

Sole

With A, ch 8.

Rnd 1: Sc in 2nd ch from hook and in each ch across to last ch, 4 hdc in last ch; working in free loops of beginning ch, sc in next 5 chs, 3 sc in next ch, join with sl st to first sc. (18 sts)

Rnd 2: Ch1, sc in same st as joining st and in next 3 sts, hdc in next 2 sts, 2 dc in each of next 4 sts, hdc in next 2 sts, sc in next 3 sts, 2 sc in each of last 3 sts, join with sl st to first sc. st (25 sts)

Rnd 3: Ch 2 (this ch-2 is not considered a stitch), hdc in same st as joining st and in next 6 sts, 2 hdc in next st, (hdc in next st, 2 hdc in next st) 3 times, hdc in next 5 sts, (sc in next sc, 2 sc in next st) 3 times, join with sl st to first hdc. (32 sts)

Boot

Rnd 4: Ch 1, working in BLO (see Stitch Guide, page 98), sc in each st around, join with sl st to the first sc.
Rnd 5: Ch 1, sc in each st around, join with sl st to the first sc.
Rnd 6: Ch 1, sc in same st as joining st and in next 3 sts, sc2tog, hdc2tog, (dc2tog) 6 times, hdc2tog, sc2tog, sc in each st to end of rnd, join with sl st to first sc. (22 sts)
Rnd 7: Ch 1, sc in same st as joining st and in next 3 sts, hdc2tog, (dc2tog) 3, hdc2tog, sc in each st to end of rnd, join with sl st to first sc. (17 sts)
Rnd 8: Ch 2, hdc in each st around to last 2 sts, hdc2tog, join with sl st to first hdc. (16 hdc)
Fasten off A. Join with color B.

Cuff

Rnd 9: Ch 1, sc in each st around, join with sl st to first sc.
Fasten off B. Join with color C.
Rnd 10: Ch 1, sc in each st around, join with sl st to first sc.
Fasten off.

Size 6–9 Months:

Sole

With A, ch 10.
Rnd 1: Sc in 2nd ch from hook and in each ch across to last ch, 4 hdc in last ch; working in free loops of beginning ch, sc in next 7 chs, 3 sc in next ch, join with sl st to first sc. (22 sts)

Rnd 2: Ch1, sc in same st as joining st and in next 5 sts, hdc in next 2 sts, 2 dc in each of next 4 sts, hdc in next 2 sts, sc in next 5 sts, 2 sc in each of last 3 sts, join with sl st to first sc. (29 sts)
Rnd 3: Ch 2 (this ch-2 is not considered a stitch) hdc in same st as joining and in next 8 sts, 2 hdc in next st, (hdc in next st, 2 hdc in next st) 3 times, hdc in next 7 sts, (sc in next sc, 2 sc in next st) 3 times, join with sl st to first hdc. (36 sts)

Boot

Rnd 4: Ch 1, working in BLO (see Stitch Guide, page 98), sc in each st around, join with sl st to the first sc.
Rnd 5: Ch 1, sc in each st around, join with sl st to the first sc.
Rnd 6: Ch 1, sc in same st as joining st and in next 5 sts, sc2tog, hdc2tog, (dc2tog) 6 times, hdc2tog, sc2tog, sc in each st to end, join with sl st to first sc. (26 sts)
Rnd 7: Ch 1, sc in same st as joining and in next 5 sts, hdc2tog, (dc2tog) 3 times, hdc2tog, sc in each st to end, join with sl st to first sc. (21 sts)
Rnd 8: Ch 2, hdc in each st around to last 2 sts, hdc2tog, join with sl st to first hdc. (20 hdc)
Fasten off A. Join with color B.

Cuff

Rnd 9: Ch 1, sc in each st around, join with sl st to first sc.
Fasten off B. Join with color C.
Rnd 10: Ch 1, sc in each st around, join with sl st to first sc.
Fasten off.

MAISIE
SET

BLANKET, HAT, BOOTIES

Let the color run wild with this set by using a variegated yarn! It will make a unique Blanket, Hat, and Bootie set for the wee one!

BLANKET

Yarn
Premier Yarns Colorfusion DK; light weight #3; 100% acrylic; 3.5 oz (100 g) / 325 yd (298 m) per skein:
- 1196-13 Salt Water Taffy, 4 balls

Hook and Other Materials
- US size G-6 (4 mm) crochet hook
- Yarn needle

Finished Measurements
Width: 35 in (89 cm)
Length: 36 in (91.6 cm)

Gauge
14 dc x 10 rows = 4 in (10.2 cm) in pattern

INSTRUCTIONS
Ch 130.

Row 1: Dc in 4th ch from hook and in each st across, turn. (128 dc)

Rows 2–12: Ch 3 (this counts as a double crochet here and throughout), dc in each st across, turn.

Row 13: Ch 3, dc in next 5 sts, *2 dc in next st, sk 1 st; rep from * across to last 6 sts, dc in last 6 sts, turn.

Row 14: Ch 3, dc in next 5 sts, sk 1 st, 2 dc in sp between last skipped st and next st, *sk 2 sts, 2 dc in sp between last skipped st and next st; rep from * across to last 6 sts, dc in last 6 sts, turn.

Rep Row 14 until blanket measures 31 in (78.8 cm).

Last 12 Rows: Ch 3, dc in each st across, turn.

Fasten off. Weave in ends.

BOOTIES

Yarn

Premier Yarns Colorfusion DK; light weight #3; 100% acrylic; 3.5 oz (100 g) / 325 yd (298 m) per skein
- 1196-13 Salt Water Taffy, 1 ball

Hook and Other Materials
- US size G-6 (4 mm) crochet hook
- Yarn needle

Finished Measurements
3–6 Months (9–12 Months)
Width: 2 (2) in / 5.1 (5.1) cm
Height: 3 (3½) in / 7.7 (9) cm

Gauge
20 sc x 20 rows = 4 in (10.2 cm)

INSTRUCTIONS

Size 3–6 Months:

Sole
With A, ch 8.
Rnd 1: Sc in 2nd ch from hook and in each ch across to last ch, 4 hdc in last ch, working in free loops of beginning ch, sc in next 5 chs, 3 sc in next ch, join with sl st to first sc. (18 sts)
Rnd 2: Ch1, sc in same st as joining st and in next 3 sts, hdc in next 2 sts, 2 dc in each of next 4 sts, hdc in next 2 sts, sc in next 3 sts, 2 sc in each of last 3 sts, join with sl st to first sc. (25 sts)
Rnd 3: Ch 2 (this ch-2 is not considered a stitch), hdc in same st as joining st and in next 6 sts, 2 hdc in next st, (hdc in next st, 2 hdc in next st) 3 times, hdc in next 5 sts, (sc in next sc, 2 sc in next st) 3 times, join with sl st to first hdc. (32 sts)

Boot
Rnd 4: Ch 1, working in BLO (see Stitch Guide, page 98), sc in each st around, join with sl st to the first sc.
Rnd 5: Ch 1, sc in each st around, join with sl st to the first sc.
Rnd 6: Ch 1, sc in same st as joining and in next 3 sts, sc2tog, hdc2tog, (dc2tog) 6 times, hdc2tog, sc2tog, sc in each st to end, join with sl st to first sc. (22 sts)
Rnd 7: Ch 1, sc in same st as joining st and in next 3 sts, hdc2tog, (dc2tog) 3 times, hdc2tog, sc in each st to end, join with sl st to first sc. (17 sts)
Rnd 8: Ch 2, hdc in each st around to last 2 sts, hdc2tog, join with sl st to first hdc. (16 hdc)
Fasten off A. Join with color B.

Cuff
Rnd 9: Ch 3 (this counts as the first double crochet in this row), dc in same st, sk 1 st, *2 dc in next st, sk 1 st; rep from * around, join with sl st to 3rd ch of beg ch-3.
Rnd 10: Sl st to sp between next 2 dc, ch 3, dc in same sp, *2 dc in sp between each 2dc sets, join with sl st to 3rd ch of beg ch-3.
Rnds 11 and 12: Rep Rnd 10.
Fasten off. Weave in ends.

Size 9–12 Months:

Sole
With A, ch 10.
Rnd 1: Sc in 2nd ch from hook and in each ch across to last ch, 4 hdc in last ch, working in free loops of beginning ch, sc in next 7 chs, 3 sc in next ch, join with sl st to first sc. (22 sts)
Rnd 2: Ch1, sc in same st as joining st and in next 5 sts, hdc in next 2 sts, 2 dc in each of next 4 sts, hdc in next 2 sts, sc in next 5 sts, 2 sc in each of last 3 sts, join with sl st to first sc. (29 sts)

Rnd 3: Ch 2 (this ch-2 is not considered a stitch here and throughout), hdc in same st as joining and in next 8 sts, 2 hdc in next st, (hdc in next st, 2 hdc in next st) 3 times, hdc in next 7 sts, (sc in next sc, 2 sc in next st) 3 times, join with sl st to first st hdc. (36 sts)

Boot

Rnd 4: Ch 1, working in BLO (see Stitch Guide, page 98), sc in each st around, join with sl st to the first sc.

Rnd 5: Ch 1, sc in each st around, join with sl st to the first sc.

Rnd 6: Ch 1, sc in same st as joining st and in next 5 sts, sc2tog, hdc2tog, (dc2tog) 6 times, hdc2tog, sc2tog, sc in each st to end, join with sl st to first sc. (26 sts)

Rnd 7: Ch 1, sc in same st as joining and in next 5 sts, hdc2tog, (dc2tog) 3 times, hdc2tog, sc in each st to end, join with sl st to first sc. (21 sts)

Rnd 8: Ch 2, hdc in each st around to last 2 sts, hdc2tog, join with sl st to first hdc. (20 hdc)

Cuff

Rnd 9: Ch 3 (this counts as a double cro-chet in this row), dc in same st, sk 1 st, *2 dc in next st, sk 1 st; rep from * around, join with sl st to ch-3 of beg ch-3.

Rnd 10: Sl st to sp between next 2 dc, ch 3, dc in same sp, *2 dc in sp between each 2dc sets, join with sl st to ch-3 of beg ch-3.

Rnds 11 and 12: Rep Rnd 10.
Fasten off. Weave in ends.

HAT

Yarn

Premier Yarns Colorfusion DK; light weight #3; 100% acrylic; 3.5 oz (100 g) / 325 yd (298 m) per skein
- 1196-13 Salt Water Taffy, 1 ball

Hook and Other Materials
- US size G-6 (4 mm) crochet hook
- Yarn needle

Finished Measurements

3–6 Months (9–12 Months)
Circumference: 16 (18) in / 40.7 (45.8) cm
Height: 5¾ (6½) in / 14.7 (16.7) cm

Gauge

20 sc x 24 rows = 4 in (10.2 cm)

INSTRUCTIONS

Create a magic ring (see Stitch Guide, page 94).

Rnd 1: 10 (12) sc in ring, join with sl st to first sc. 10 (12) sc

Rnd 2: Ch 4 (this stitch counts as the first double crochet and ch-1 stitch of this row), (dc, ch 1) in each st around, join with sl st to ch-3 of beg ch-4. 10 (12) dc, 10 (12) ch-1 sps

Rnd 3: Sl st in next ch-1 sp, ch 3 (counts as a double crochet stitch for this row), 2 dc in same sp, 3 dc in each ch-1 sp, join with sl st in 3rd ch of beg ch-3. 30 (36) dc

Rnd 4: Ch 1, *sc in next 5 (4) sts, ch 1; rep from * around, join with sl st to first sc. 30 (36) sts, 10 (10) ch-1 sps

Rnd 5: Sl st to next ch-1 sp, ch 6 (counts as double crochet and ch-3 stitch for this row), dc in same sp, sk 3 sts, *(dc, ch 3, dc) in next ch-1 sp, sk 3 sts; rep from * around, join with sl st to 3rd ch of beg ch-6.

Rnd 6: *(Sl st to next ch-3 sp, ch 1, 5 dc in same ch-3 sp, ch 1, sl st in same ch-3 sp), rep from * around, join with sl st to first sl st at beginning of round. 10 (12 petals)

Rnd 7: Sl st on side of dc, sc in top of next 2 dc, ch 1, sk 1 st, sc in next 2 dc, ch 1, *sc in next 2 dc, ch 1, sk 1, sc in next 2 dc, ch 1; rep from * around; join with sl st to first sc.

Rnd 8: Sl st to next ch-1 sp, ch 4 (counts as first dc and ch-1), dc in same sp, (dc, ch 1, dc) in each ch-1 sp around.

Rep Rnd 8 until hat measures 5¼ (6) in / 13.3 (15.24) cm.

Last rnd: Sl st to next ch-3 sp, ch 1, *7 dc in same sp, ch 1, sl in next ch-3 sp; rep from * around, join with sl st to first dc. Fasten off. Weave in ends.

POPPY
SET

BLANKET, HAT, BOOTIES

By using a pre-made box of colors, you can mix and match your set until you get the look you want. Another option is to use scrap yarn and have fun with all of the stripes!

BLANKET

Yarn
Premier Yarns Color Pack Box 2; light
  weight #3; 100% acrylic; 0.7 oz (20 g) /
  54 yd (50 m) per skein; 14 oz (400 g) /
  1,080 yd (1,000 m) per box
- Box 2, 1 pack

Hook and Other Materials
- US size 7 (4.5 mm) crochet hook
- Yarn needle

Finished Measurements
Width: 28½ in (72.5 cm)
Length: 28½ in (72.5 cm)

Gauge
3 shells = 3 in (7.7 cm)
7 rows = 3½ in (9 cm)

Color Sequence
Working in any order of the mini skein colors, change colors every 2 rows.

INSTRUCTIONS
With first color, ch 159.

Row 1: (2 dc, ch 2, 2 dc) in 6th ch from hook, *sk next 5 chs, (2 dc, ch 2, 2 dc) in next ch; rep from * across to last 3 chs, sk 2 chs, dc in last ch, turn.

Row 2: Ch 1, sc in first dc, *ch 3, dc in next ch-2 sp, ch 3, sk next 2 dc, sc between last skipped dc and next dc; rep from * across, ending with last sc at top of turn-ing ch, turn. Fasten off. Join next color.

Row 3: Ch 4 (this counts as the first treble stitch of this row), sk next ch-3 sp, (2 dc, ch 2, 2 dc) in next dc, *sk next 2 ch-3 sps, (2 dc, ch 2, 2 dc) in next dc; rep from * across to last ch-3 sp, sk next ch-3 sp, tr in last sc, turn.

Rep Rows 2 and 3 until pattern measures 28½ in (72.5 cm).

Fasten off. Weave in ends.

BOOTIES

Yarn
Premier Yarns Color Pack Box 2; light
  weight #3; 100% acrylic; 0.7 oz (20 g) /
  54 yd (50 m) per skein; 14 oz (400 g) /
  1,080 yd (1,000 m) per box
• Box 2, 1 pack

Hook and Other Materials
• US size G-6 (4 mm) crochet hook
• Yarn needle

Finished Measurements
3–6 Months (6–9 Months)
Width: 2 (2) in / 5 (5 cm)
Height: 3 (3½) in / 7.7 (9) cm

Gauge
20 sc x 20 rows = 4 in (10.2 cm)

Special Stitches
Cluster: (Yarn over and draw up a loop,
  yarn over and draw through 2 loops
  on hook) 3 times. Yarn over and draw
  through all 4 loops on hook.

INSTRUCTIONS

Size 3–6 Months:

Sole
With first color, ch 8.
Rnd 1: Sc in second ch from hook and in
  each ch across to last ch, 4 hdc in last ch,
  working in free loops of beginning ch, sc
  in next 5 chs, 3 sc in next ch, join with sl
  st to first sc. (18 sts)
Rnd 2: Ch1, sc in same st as joining st and in
  next 3 sts, hdc in next 2 sts, 2 dc in each
  of next 4 sts, hdc in next 2 sts, sc in next
  3 sts, 2 sc in each of last 3 sts, join with sl
  st to first sc. (25 sts)

Rnd 3: Ch 2 (this ch-2 is not considered a
  stitch), hdc in same st as joining st and in
  next 6 sts, 2 hdc in next st, (hdc in next
  st, 2 hdc in next st) 3 times, hdc in next 5
  sts, (sc in next sc, 2 sc in next st) 3 times,
  join with sl st to first hdc. (32 sts)

Boot
Rnd 4: Ch 1, working in BLO (see Stitch
  Guide, page 98), sc in each st around,
  join with sl st in first sc.
Rnd 5: Ch 1, sc in each st around, join with
  sl st to first sc.
Rnd 6: Ch 1, sc in same st as joining st and
  in next 3 sts, sc2tog, hdc2tog, (dc2tog)
  6 times, hdc2tog, sc2tog, sc in each st to
  end, join with sl st to first sc. (22 sts)
Rnd 7: Ch 1, sc in same st as joining st and
  in next 3 sts, hdc2tog, (dc2tog) 3 times,
  hdc2tog, sc in each st to end, join with sl
  st to first sc. (17 sts)
Rnd 8: Ch 2, hdc in each st around to last
  2 sts, hdc2tog, join with sl st to first hdc.
  (16 hdc)
Fasten off A, join B.

Cuff
Rnd 9: Ch 2 (this ch-2 is not considered a
  stitch), dc in same st, cluster in each st
  around, join with sl st to first dc.
Fasten off. Join next color.
Rnd 10: Ch 1, sc in each st around, join with
  sl st to first sc.
Fasten off. Join next color.
Rnd 11: Rep Rnd 9.
Fasten off. Join first color.
Rnd 12: Rep Rnd 10.
Fasten off. Weave in ends.

Size 6–9 Months:

Sole

With first color, ch 10.

Rnd 1: Sc in second ch from hook and in each ch across to last ch, 4 hdc in last ch, working in free loops of beginning ch, sc in next 7 chs, 3 sc in next ch, join with sl st to first sc. (22 sts)

Rnd 2: Ch1, sc in same st as joining st and in next 5 sts, hdc in next 2 sts, 2 dc in each of next 4 sts, hdc in next 2 sts, sc in next 5 sts, 2 sc in each of last 3 sts, join with sl st to first sc. (29 sts)

Rnd 3: Ch 2 (this ch-2 is not considered a stitch), hdc in same st as joining st and in next 8 sts, 2 hdc in next st, (hdc in next st, 2 hdc in next st) 3 times, hdc in next 7 sts, (sc in next sc, 2 sc in next st) 3 times, join with sl st to first hdc. (36 sts)

Boot

Rnd 4: Ch 1, working in BLO (see Stitch Guide, page 98), sc in each st around, join with sl st to the first sc.

Rnd 5: Ch 1, sc in each st around, join with sl st to the first sc.

Rnd 6: Ch 1, sc in same st as joining st and in next 5 sts, sc2tog, hdc2tog, (dc2tog) 6 times, hdc2tog, sc2tog, sc in each st to end, join with sl st to first sc. (26 sts)

Rnd 7: Ch 1, sc in same st as joining st and in next 5 sts, hdc2tog, (dc2tog) 3 times, hdc2tog, sc in each st to end, join with sl st to first sc. (21 sts)

Rnd 8: Ch 2, hdc in each st around to last 2 sts, hdc2tog, join with sl st to first hdc. (20 hdc) Fasten off. Join next color.

Cuff

Rnd 9: Ch 2 (this ch-2 is not considered a stitch), dc in same st, cluster in each st around, join with sl st to first dc.
Fasten off, join next color.

Rnd 10: Ch 1, sc in each st around, join with sl st to first sc.
Fasten off. Join next color.

Rnd 11: Rep Rnd 9.
Fasten off. Join first color.

Rnd 12: Rep Rnd 10.
Fasten off. Weave in ends.

HAT

Yarn

Premier Yarns Color Pack Box 2; light weight #3; 100% acrylic; 0.7 oz (20 g) / 54 yd (50 m) per skein; 14 oz (400 g) / 1,080 yd (1,000 m) per box
- Box 2, 1 pack

Hook and Other Materials

- US size G-6 (4 mm) crochet hook
- Yarn needle

Finished Measurements

Newborn (3–6 Months, 9–12 Months)
Circumference: 14 (16, 18) in / 35.5 (40.7, 45.8) cm
Height: 5 (5¾, 6½) in / 12.7 (14.7, 16.6) cm

Gauge

16 sc x 13 rows = 4 in (10.2 cm) in pattern

Color Sequence

Change colors each round in any order from the Color Pack.

Special Stitches

Cluster: (Yarn over and draw up a loop, yarn over and draw through 2 loops on hook) 3 times. Yarn over and draw through all loops on hook.

INSTRUCTIONS

With first color, create a magic ring (see Stitch Guide, page 94).

Rnd 1: Ch 2 (this ch-2 is not considered a stitch), 10 (10, 12) clusters (see Special Stitches) in ring, join with sl st to first dc–10 (10, 12) sts. Fasten off. Join next color.

Rnd 2: Ch 1, 2 sc in each st around, join with sl st to first sc. 20 (20, 24) sts. Fasten off. Join next color.

Rnd 3: Ch 2 (this ch-2 is not considered a stitch), *cluster in next st, (cluster, ch 1) in next st; rep from * around, join with sl st to first cluster. 30 (30, 36) sts. Fasten off. Join next color.

Rnd 4: *Note: use each st and ch-1 sp.* Ch 1, *sc in next 2 sts, 2 sc in next st; rep from * around, join with sl st to first sc. 40 (40, 48) sc. Fasten off. Join next color.

Rnd 5: Ch 2 (this ch-2 is not considered a stitch), *cluster in next 3 sts, (cluster, ch 1) in next st; rep from * around, join with sl st to first cluster. 50 (50, 60) sts. Fasten off. Join next color.

3–6 Months and 9–12 Months only:

Rnd 6: Ch 1, sc in each st around, join with sl st to first sc. Fasten off. Join next color.

Rnd 7: Ch 2 (this ch-2 is not considered a stitch), cluster in next 4 sts, (cluster, ch 1) in next st; rep from * around, join with sl st to first cluster (60, 72) sts. Fasten off. Join next color.

All sizes:

Rnd 6 (8, 8): Ch 1, sc in each st around, join with sl st to first sc. Fasten off. Join next color.

Rnd 7 (9, 9): Ch 2 (this ch-2 is not considered a stitch), cluster in each st around, join with sl st to first cluster. Fasten off. Join next color.

Next rnd: Ch 1, sc in next 3 (4, 4) sts, sc2tog; rep from * around, join with sl st to first st. 40 (50, 60) sts. Do not fasten off color.

Last rnd: Ch 1, sc in each st around. Fasten off. Weave in ends.

REMY
SET

NO-SCRATCH MITTS, HIGH-LOW CARDIGAN, HAT

Keep your baby cozy with this sweet set. With their head, hands, and body covered, your little one will be the warmest (and cutest!).

NO-SCRATCH MITTS

Yarn
Premier Yarns Everyday Dots; light weight #3; 100% anti-pilling acrylic; 3.5 oz (100 g) / 273 yd (250 m) per ball
- 1195-08 Sleepytime, 1 ball

Hook and Other Materials
- US size G-6 (4 mm) crochet hook
- Yarn needle

Finished Measurements
One size: Newborn
Diameter: 2½ in (6.4 cm)
Circumference: 5 in (12.8 cm)
Height: 3 in (7.7 cm)

Gauge
20 dc x 14 rows = 4 in (10.2 cm) in pattern

INSTRUCTIONS
Create a magic ring (see Stitch Guide, page 94).

Rnd 1: Ch 2 (this ch-2 is not considered a stitch here and throughout), 12 dc in ring, join with sl st to first dc. (12 dc)

Rnd 2: Ch 2, *dc in next st, 2 dc in next st, join with sl st to first dc. (18 dc)

Rnd 3: Ch 2, *dc in next 2 sts, 2 dc in next st, join with sl st to first dc. (24 dc)

Rnds 4–6: Ch 2, dc in each st around, join with sl st to first dc. (24 dc)

Rnd 7: Ch 2, *dc in next st, dc2tog; rep from * around, join with sl st to first dc. (16 dc)

Rnd 8: Ch 2, dc in each st around, join with sl st to first dc. (16 dc)

Rnd 9: Ch 2, *sc in next st, ch 3; rep from * around, join with sl st to first sc. 16 sc, 16 ch-3 sps. Fasten off.

Tie

Ch 32. Fasten off.

Weave Tie in and out of Rnd 8 and tie in a bow.

Weave in ends.

HIGH-LOW CARDIGAN

Yarn

Premier Yarns Everyday Dots; light weight #3; 100% anti-pilling acrylic; 3.5 oz (100 g) / 273 yd (250 m) per ball

• 1195-08 Sleepytime, 2 balls

Hook and Other Materials

• US size 7 (4.5 mm) crochet hook
• Yarn needle

Finished Measurements

3–6 Months (9–12 Months)

Chest: 18 (18½) in / 45.8 (47.1) cm

Total Length: 9 (9¾) in / 22.8 (24.8) cm

Gauge

20 hdc x 14 rows = 4 in (10.2 cm)

Pattern Note

• The cardigan is made from sleeve end to opposite sleeve end (sideways), folded and sewn to complete.

INSTRUCTIONS

Sleeve 1

Ch 31 (35).

Row 1 (RS): Hdc in 2nd ch from hook and in each ch across, turn. 30 (34) hdc.

Row 2: Ch 2 (counts as half double crochet here and throughout), hdc in each st across, turn.

Rep Row 2 until Sleeve measures 7 (7½) in / 7.8 (9.2) cm ending on a WS row.

Fasten off.

Body, Part 1

Row 1 (RS): Ch 30 (34), turn (creates beg ch of left side for Cardigan front), hdc 30 (34) across Sleeve, ch 31, 35 (creates beg ch of Cardigan back), turn. 30 (34) hdc, 2 ch sections

Row 2: Hdc in 2nd ch from hook and in each ch across, hdc 30 (34) across Sleeve, hdc in each ch across, turn. 90 (102) hdc

Row 3: Ch 2, hdc in each st across, turn.

Rep Row 3 for a total of 4¼ (4½) in / 10.8 (11.5) cm for Body, Part 1, ending on a WS row.

Middle Back

Row 1 (RS): Ch 2, hdc in next 60 (68) sts, turn. 60 (68) hdc

Row 2: Ch 2, hdc in each st across, turn.

Body, Part 2

Row 3 (RS): Ch 2, hdc in next 60 (68 sts), ch 31 (35), turn. 60 (68) hdc, 31 (35) chs

Row 4: Ch 2, hdc in 2nd ch from hook and in each ch across, hdc in each st across, turn. 90 (102) hdc

Row 5: Ch 2, hdc in each st across, turn.

Rep Row 5 for a total of 4¼ (4½) in / 10.8 (11.5) cm for Body, Part 2, ending on a WS row (*Note: should be same row count as Body, Part 1*).

Fasten off.

Sleeve 2

Row 1 (WS): With WS facing, join yarn in st 30 (34), ch 2, hdc in next 30 (34) sts, leaving rem sts unworked, turn. 30 (34) hdc

Row 2: Ch 2, hdc in each st across, turn.
Rep Row 2 until Sleeve measures 7 (7½) in / 7.8 (9.2) cm, ending on a WS row. *(Note: should be same row counts as Sleeve 1).*
Fasten off. Fold panel in half and sew under sleeves and sides.

Sleeve Cuffs

Rnd 1: Join yarn in seam, ch 2 (this ch-2 is not considered a stitch here and throughout) using ends of rows as sts, dc in each st around, join with sl st to first dc (not ch-2 sp).

Rnd 2: Ch 2, *fpdc (see Stitch Guide, page 108) on next st, bpdc (see Stitch Guide, page 109) on next st; rep from * around, join with sl st to first fpdc.

Rnds 3 and 4: Rep Rnd 2.
Fasten off.

HAT

Yarn

Premier Yarns Everyday Dots; light weight #3; 100% anti-pilling acrylic; 3.5 oz (100 g) / 273 yd (250 m) per ball
- 1195-08 Sleepytime, 1 ball

Hook and Other Materials

- US size F-5 (3.75 mm) crochet hook
- Yarn needle

Finished Measurements

Newborn (3–6 Months, 9–12 Months)
Circumference: 14 (16, 18) in / 35.7 (40.7, 45.8) cm
Height: 5 (5¾, 6½) in / 12.8 (14.7/16.6) cm

Gauge

20 dc x 14 rows = 4 in (10.2 cm) in pattern

INSTRUCTIONS

All sizes:
Create a magic ring (see Stitch Guide, page 94).

Rnd 1: Ch 3, 9 dc in ring, join with sl st to first dc. (10 dc)

Rnd 2: Ch 2 (this ch-2 is not considered a stitch here and throughout), 2 dc in each st around, join with sl st to first dc. (20 dc)

Rnd 3: Ch 2, *dc in next st, 2 dc in next st, join with sl st to first dc. (30 dc)

Rnd 4: Ch 2, *dc in next 2 sts, 2 dc in next st, join with sl st to first dc. (40 dc)

Rnd 5: Ch 2, *dc in next 3 sts, 2 dc in next st, join with sl st to first dc. (50 dc)

3–6 Months and 9–12 Months only:
Rnd 6: Ch 2, *dc in next 4 sts, 2 dc in next st, join with sl st to first dc. (60 dc)

9–12 Months only:
Rnd 7: Ch 2, *dc in next 5 sts, 2 dc in next st, join with sl st to first dc. (70 dc)

Body

All sizes:
Rnd 1: Ch 2 (this ch-2 is not considered a stitch here and throughout), *dc in next 4 sts, fpdc (see Stitch Guide, page 108); rep from * around, join with sl st to first dc.

Rnd 2: Ch 2, dc in next 3 sts, fpdc in next st, *dc in next 4 sts, fpdc; rep from * until 1 st remains, dc in last st, join with sl st to first dc.

Rnd 3: Ch 2, dc in next 2 sts, fpdc in next st, *dc in next 4 sts, fpdc; rep from * until 2 sts remain, dc in last 2 sts, join with sl st to first dc.

Rnd 4: Ch 2, dc in next st, fpdc in next st, *dc in next 4 sts, fpdc; rep from * until 3 sts remain, dc in last 3 sts, join with sl st to first dc.

Rnd 5: Ch 2, *fpdc on next st, dc in next 4 sts; rep from * around, join with sl st to first dc.

Rep Rnds 1–5 until hat measures 4¾ (5½, 6) in / 12.1 (14, 15.3) cm.

Next rnd: Ch 2, hdc in each st around, join with sl st to first hdc.

Next 2 rnds: Ch 2, working in the 3rd lp of hdc (see Stitch Guide, page 101), hdc in each st around, join with sl st sl to first hdc.

Fasten off. Weave in ends.

THEO
SET

SOCKS, HAT, VEST

Stitch your little one a sweet set—coordinated from head to toe!

SOCKS

Yarn
Premier Yarns Anti-Pilling Everyday DK;
  light weight #3; 100% anti-pilling acrylic;
  3.5 oz (100 g) / 273 yd (250 m) per ball
- 1070-02 Cream, 1 ball

Hook and Other Materials
- US size C-2 (2.75 mm) crochet hook
- Yarn needle

Finished Measurements
Toe to back of heel:
3–6 Months: 3½ in (8.8 cm)
9–12 Months: 4 in (10.2 cm)

Gauge
16 sc x 16 rows = 4 in (10.2 cm)

INSTRUCTIONS

Size 3–6 Months:

Toe/Foot
Ch 2.
Rnd 1: 8 sc in 2nd ch from hook, do not
  join. (8 sts)
Rnd 2: Working in rounds, 2 sc in each st.
  (16 sts)
Rnd 3: (Sc in next st, 2 sc in next st)
  around. (24 sts)
Rnd 4: (Sc in next 2 sts, 2 sc in next st)
  around. (32 sts)
Rnds 5–22: Sc in each st around.

Heel
Row 23: Sc in next 16 sts, leaving remaining sts unworked, turn. (16 sts)
Rows 24–28: Ch 1, sc in each st across, turn.
Row 29: Ch 1, sc in next 4 sts, sc2tog 4 times, sc in next 4 sts, turn. (12 sts)
Row 30: Ch 1, sc in next 4 sts, sc2tog 2 times, sc in next 4 sts. (10 sts)

Ankle
Rnd 31: Sl st to the first st of rnd, ch 1, using ends of rows as sts, sc 8, sc 16 across Foot, using ends of rows as sts, sc 8, join with sl st to first sc. (32 sts)
Rnd 32: Ch 1, sc in each st around, join with sl st to first sc. (32 sts)

Cuff
Rnd 33: Ch 3, dc around st just made, sk 1 st, *dc in next st, dc around front post just made (see Stitch Guide, page 108), sk 1 st; rep from * around, join with sl st in ch-3 of beg ch-3.
Rnd 34: Ch 1, sc in each ch and st around, join with sl st to first sc.
Rnds 35 and 36: Rep Rnds 33 and 34.
Fasten off. Sew heel closed with yarn needle. Weave in ends.

Size 9–12 Months:

Toe/Foot
Ch 2.
Rnd 1: 8 sc in second ch from hook, do not join. (8 sts)
Rnd 2: Working in rnds, 2 sc in each st around. (16 sts)
Rnd 3: (Sc in next st, 2 sc in next st) around. (24 sts)
Rnd 4: (Sc in next 2 sts, 2 sc in next st) around. (32 sts)
Rnd 5: (Sc in next 7 sts, 2 sc in next st around. (36 sts)
Rnds 6–26: Sc in each st around.

Heel
Row 27: Sc in next 18 sts, leaving remaining sts unworked, turn. (18 sts)
Rows 28–32: Ch 1, sc in each st across, turn.
Row 33: Ch 1, sc in next 5 sts, sc2tog 4 times, sc in next 5 sts, turn. (14 sts)
Row 34: Ch 1, sc in next 5 sts, sc2tog 2 times, sc in next 5 sts. (12 sts)

Ankle
Rnd 35: Sl st to the first st sc of previous rnd, ch 1, using ends of rows as sts, sc 8, sc 18 across Foot, using ends of rows as sts, sc 8, join with sl st to first sc. (34 sts)
Rnd 36: Ch 1, sc in each st around, join with sl st to first sc. (34 sts)

Cuff
Rnd 37: Ch 3, dc in st just made, sk 1 st, *dc in next st, dc around front post just made (see Stitch Guide, page 108), sk 1 st; rep from * around, join with sl st in ch-3 of beg ch-3.
Rnd 38: Ch 1, sc in each ch and st around, join with sl st in ch-3 of beg ch-3.
Rnds 39 and 40: Rep Rnds 37 and 38.
Fasten off. Sew heel closed with yarn needle. Weave in ends.

HAT

Yarn
Premier Yarns Anti-Pilling Everyday DK; light weight #3; 100% anti-pilling acrylic; 3.5 oz (100 g) / 273 yd (250 m) per skein
- A: 107062 Meadow, 1 ball
- B: 1070-02 Cream, 1 ball

Hook and Other Materials
- US size 7 (4.5 mm) crochet hook
- Yarn needle

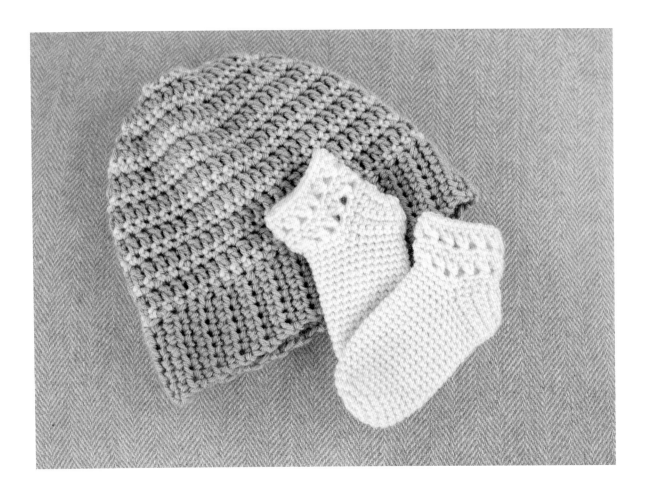

Finished Measurements
Newborn (3–6 Months, 9–12 Months)
Circumference: 14 (16, 18) in / 35.6 (40.7, 45.8) cm
Height: 5 (5¾, 6½) in / 12.7 (14.7, 16.6) cm

Gauge
20 dc x 16 rows = 4 in (10.2 cm)

Pattern Notes
• Hat is made by creating the Brim first in back-and-forth rows and then creating the Body on the ends of the rows of one side.
• To change yarn color, work last stitch of old color to last yarn-over step. Yarn over with new color and draw through all loops on hook to complete the stitch.

Work over the strand of old color as you work each row. See also Stitch Guide, page 110.

INSTRUCTIONS

Brim
With A, ch 8.
Row 1: Sc in 2nd ch from hook and in each ch across, turn. (7 sc)
Row 2: Ch 1, hdc in each st across, turn.
Row 3: Ch 1, sc in each st across, turn.
Row 4: Ch 1, hdc in each st across, turn.
Rows 5–54 (60, 66): Rep Rows 3 and 4.
Fold Brim and sl st short ends together. Fasten off.

Body
Rnd 1: Join color B, ch 1, working in the ends of rows, sc in each st around, join with sl st in first sc at beg of rnd. 54 (60, 66) sc

Fasten off. Join color A.

Rnd 2: Ch 3 (counts as a double crochet stitch), dc in each st around, join with sl st in first dc made at beg of rnd.

Fasten off. Join color B.

Rnd 3: Ch 1, sc in each st around, join with sl st in sc made at beg of rnd.

Fasten off. Join color A.

Rep Rnds 2 and 3 until Hat measures 5 (5¾, 6½) in / 12.8 (14.7, 16.6) cm, ending on Rnd 3.

Decrease Crown
Note: Continue to change colors every rnd in same sequence.

Rnd 1: Ch 2 (this ch-2 is not considered a stitch here and throughout), dc in next 7 (8, 9) sts, dc2tog; rep from * around, join with sl st in first dc. 48 (54, 60) dc.

Rnd 2: Ch 1, sc in next 6 (7, 8) sts, sc2tog; rep from * around, join with sl st in first sc. 42 (48, 54) sc

Rnd 3: Ch 2, dc in next 5 (6, 7) sts, dc2tog; rep from * around, join with sl st in first dc. 36 (42, 48) dc

Rnd 4: Ch 1, sc in next 4 (5, 6) sts, sc2tog; rep from * around, join with sl st in first sc. 30 (36, 42) sc

Rnd 5: Ch 2, dc in next 3 (4, 5) sts, dc2tog; rep from * around, join with sl st in first dc. 24 (30, 36) dc

Size Newborn only:
Rnd 6: Ch 1, sc in next 2 (3, 4) sts, sc2tog; rep from * around, join with sl st in first sc. 16 (24, 30) sc

Fasten off leaving a long tail.

Thread yarn needle with long tail and close last rnd.

Size 3–6 Months only:
Rnd 6: Ch 1, sc in next 2 (3, 4) sts, sc2tog; rep from * around, join with sl st in first sc. 16 (24, 30) sc

Rnd 7: Ch 2, dc in next 2 sts, dc2tog; rep from * around, join with sl st in first dc. (18 dc)

Rnd 8: Ch 1, sc in next st, sc2tog; rep from * around, join with sl st in first sc. (12 sc)

Fasten off leaving a long tail.

Thread yarn needle with long tail and close last rnd.

Size 9–12 Months only:
Rnd 6: Ch 2, dc in next 4 sts, sc2tog; rep from * around, join with sl st in first dc. (30 sc)

Rnd 7: Ch 1, sc in next 3 sts, sc2tog; rep from * around, join with sl st in first sc. (24 sc)

Rnd 8: Ch 2, dc in next 2 sts, dc2tog; rep from * around, join with sl st in first dc. (18 dc)

Rnd 9: Ch 1, sc in next st, sc2tog; rep from * around, join with sl st in first sc. (12 sc)

Rnd 10: Ch 2, dc2tog 6 times, join with sl st in first dc. (6 dc)

Fasten off leaving a long tail. Thread yarn needle with long tail and close last rnd.

VEST

Yarn

Premier Yarns Anti-Pilling Everyday DK;
light weight #3; 100% anti-pilling acrylic;
3.5 oz (100 g) / 273 yd (250 m) per ball
- A: 107062 Meadow, 1 ball
- B: 1070-19 Linen, 1 ball

Hook and Other Materials
- US size 7 (4.5 mm) crochet hook
- Yarn needle

Finished Measurements

3–6 Months (6–12 Months)
Chest: 17 (18) in / 433 (45.8) cm
Length: 12 (12½) in / 306 (31.8) cm

Gauge

20 sc x 24 rows = 4 in (10.2 cm)

INSTRUCTIONS

Lower Panel

With A, ch 79 (83).

Row 1: Sc in 2nd ch from hook and in each ch across, turn. 78 (82) sc

Row 2: Ch 1, sc in each st across, turn.

Rows 3 and 4: Rep Row 2.

Fasten off. Join with color B.

Rows 5 and 6: Ch 1, sc in each st across, turn.

Fasten off. Join with color A.

Rows 7 and 8: Ch 1, sc in each st across, turn.

Fasten off. Join with color B.

Rows 9 and 10: Ch 1, sc in each st across, turn.

Fasten off. Join with color A.

Rep Row 2 until panel measures 5 (5¾) in / 12.8 (14.7) cm, end on a WS row. Fasten off. Join with color B.

Rep Row 2 until panel measures 7 (7¾) in / 17.9 (19.8) cm, end on a WS row. Do not fasten off.

Front Panel 1

Size 3–6 Months only:
Row 1 (RS): Ch 1, sc in next 15 sts, leaving rem sts unworked, turn. (15 sc)
Row 2: Ch 1, sc in each st across, turn.
Row 3: Ch 1, sc in next st, sc2tog, sc in each st across, turn. (14 sc)
Row 4: Ch 1, sc in each st across, turn.

Rows 5–20: Rep Rows 3 and 4 until you have 6 sc left in your row. (6 sc)
Fasten off leaving a long tail for sewing.

Size 6–12 Months only:
Row 1 (RS): Ch 1, sc in next 15 sts, leaving rem sts unworked, turn. (15 sc)
Rows 2–6: Ch 1, sc in each st across, turn.
Row 7 (RS): Ch 1, sc in next st, sc2tog, sc in each st across, turn. (14 sc)
Row 8: Ch 1, sc in each st across, turn.
Rows 9–24: Rep Rows 7 and 8 until you have 6 sc left in your row. (6 sc)

Row 25: Ch1, sc in each st across.
Fasten off leaving a long tail for sewing.

Back

All sizes:
Row 1: Skip 8 (9) sts on last row of Lower Panel, join yarn in next st, ch 1, sc in next 32 (34 sts), leaving rem sts unworked, turn. 32 (34) sc
Rows 2–20 (25): Ch 1, turn, sc in each st across, turn.
Fasten off.

Front Panel 2

Size 3–6 Months only:
Row 1 (RS): Sk 8 (9) sts on last row of Lower Panel, join yarn in next st, ch 1, sc in next 15 sts (no sts should be remaining), turn. (15 sc)
Row 2: Ch 1, sc in each st across, turn.
Row 3: Ch 1, sc in each st across to last 3 sts, sc2tog, sc in next st, turn. (14 sc)
Row 4: Ch 1, sc in each st across, turn.
Rows 5–20: Rep Rows 3 and 4 until you have 6 sc left in your row. (6 sc)
Fasten off leaving a long tail for sewing.

Size 6–12 Months only:
Row 1 (RS): Sk 8 (9) sts on last row of Lower Panel, join yarn in next st, ch 1, sc in next 15 sts (no sts should be remaining), turn. (15 sc)
Rows 2–7: Ch 1, sc in each st across, turn.
Row 8: Ch 1, sc in next st, sc2tog, sc in each st across, turn. (14 sc)
Row 9: Ch 1, sc in each st across, turn.

Rows 10–25: Rep Rows 8 and 9 until you have 6 sc left in your row. (6 sc)
Fasten off leaving a long tail for sewing.

Assembly

All sizes:
Sew last row of each Front Panel to Back to create shoulders.

Arm Trim

All sizes:
Rnd 1: Join with color A in bottom of arm opening, ch 1, using ends of rows as sts, sc evenly around opening, join with sl st to first sc.
Rnd 2: Ch 1, sc in each st around, join with sl st to first sc.
Fasten off.

Vest Trim

All sizes:
Rnd 1: Join color A in any bottom corner, ch 1, 3 sc in same st, work sc evenly around Vest (base, sides and around neck), working 3 sc in opposite bottom corner, join with sl st to first sc.
Rnd 2: Ch 3 (this counts as a double crochet), dc in each st around, working 3 dc in each corner, join with sl st in 3rd of beg ch-3.
Fasten off.

MOLLY
SET

ONESIE, SHORTS, BIB

Made with a #3-weight cotton, this set will be sure to be a favorite! It's cute and functional! The matching drool bib is a darling accessory that every baby needs as well as the shorts!

ONESIE

Yarn

Premier Yarns Cotton Sprout; light weight #3; 100% cotton; 3.5 oz (100 g) / 230 yd (210 m) per ball

- A: 1149-26 Cream, 1 ball
- B: 1149-20 Cadet, 1 ball
- C: 1149-28 Bark, 1 ball

Hook and Other Materials

- US size G-6 (4 mm) crochet hook
- Yarn needle

Finished Measurements

Newborn (3–6 Months, 6–9 Months)
Circumference (at Belly): 18 (20¾, 22½) in / 45.8 (52.8, 57.3) cm

Gauge

17 sc x 21 rows = 4 in (10.2 cm)

Pattern Notes

- The onesie is worked from the bottom up. Front and back bottom panel pieces are worked separately then joined and body is worked in turned-rounds to the armholes. Front and back bodice pieces are then worked separately and joined at the top with Shoulder Straps. The Flower and Tie are made separately and added to finish the piece.

INSTRUCTIONS

Back Bottom Panel

With color A, ch 17 (23, 27).

Row 1: Sc in 2nd ch from hook and each ch across, turn. 16 (22, 26) sc

Row 2: Ch 1, sc each st across, turn.

Row 3: Ch 1, sc in each st across, turn.

Row 4: Ch 1, sc in first st, 2 sc in next st, sc to last 2 sts, 2 sc in next st, sc in last st, turn. 18 (24, 28) sc

Rows 5–24 (24, 26): Rep Rows 3 and 4. 38 (44, 48) sc

Fasten off.

Front Bottom Panel

Work same as Back Bottom Panel, but do NOT fasten off.

Body

Rnd 1 (WS): Ch 1, sc across Front Bottom Panel, sc in last st worked of Back Bottom Panel, sc across Back Bottom Panel, join to first sc of Front Bottom Panel with a sl st, turn. 76 (88, 96) sc

Rnd 2 (RS): Ch 1, sc in each st around, join with a sl st to beg sc, turn.

Rnds 3–6: Ch 1, sc in each st around, join with a sl st to beg sc, turn.

Rnd 7: Ch 2, hdc in each st around, join with sl st to beg hdc, turn.

Rnds 8–21 (23, 23): Ch 1, sc in each st around, join with a sl st to beg sc, turn.

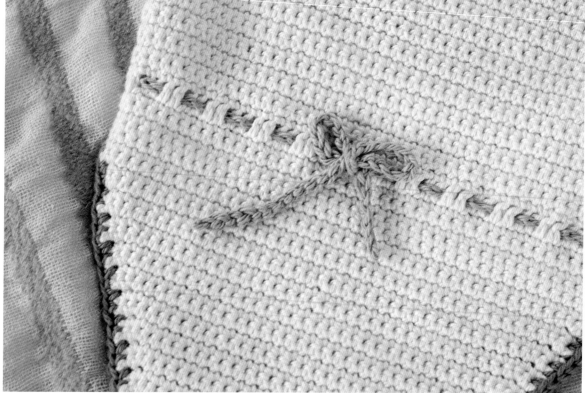

Back Bodice

Row 1 (RS): Sl st in next 2 sts, sc in next 34 (40, 44) sts, leave rem sts unworked for armhole opening and Front Bodice, turn. 34 (40, 44) sc

Row 2: Ch 1, sc in each st across, turn.

Row 3: Ch 1, sc in first st, sc2tog, sc across to last 3 sts, sc2tog, sc in last st, turn. 32 (38, 42) sc

Row 4: Ch 1, sc in each st across, turn.

Rows 5–18: Rep Rows 3 and 4. 18 (24, 28) sc Fasten off.

Front Bodice

With RS facing, join with color A in 5th unworked st after Row 1 of Back Bodice with a sl st.

Row 1 (RS): Ch 1, sc in same st, sc in next 33 (39, 43) sts, leave rem 4 sts unworked, turn. 34 (40, 44) sc

Rows 2–18: Work as for Back Bodice. 18 (24, 28) sc. Fasten off. Join with color B.

Join for Shoulder Straps

Rnd 1: Ch 8 (10, 10), sc to first st of Back Bodice to join (first shoulder strap made), sc across Back, ch 8 (10, 10), sc to first st of Front Bodice, sc across, join.

Fasten off.

Finishing

With yarn color B, sew Front and Back Bottom Panels together.

Front and Back Bottom Panel Edging

Rnd 1: With RS facing, join with color B at seam, ch 1, using ends of rows as sts, sc evenly around opening, join with sl st to beg sc.

Fasten off.

Tie

With color C, ch 110. Fasten off.

Weave in and out of hdc sts in Rnd 7 of Body. Tie.

Weave in ends.

DROOL BIB

Yarn

Premier Yarns Cotton Sprout; light weight #3; 100% cotton; 3.5 oz (100 g) / 230 yd (210 m) per ball

- 1149-28 Bark, 1 ball

Hook and Other Materials

- US size G-6 (4 mm) crochet hook
- Yarn needle

Finished Measurements

One size

From top to bottom point: 6¾ in (17.3 cm)

Gauge

Rows 1–7 = 4 in (10.2 cm) in pattern

INSTRUCTIONS

Ch 8, join with sl st to first ch to form a ring.

Row 1: Ch 3 (this counts as a double crochet here and throughout), 4 dc in ring, ch 2, 5 dc in ring, turn. 10 dc, 1 ch-2 sp

Row 2: Ch 3, dc in same st, dc in next 4 sts, (2 dc, ch 2, 2 dc) in next ch-2 sp, dc in next 4 sts, 2 dc in last st, turn. 12 dc, 1 (2 dc, ch 2, 2 dc) group

Row 3: Ch 3, dc in same st, dc in next 7 sts, (2 dc, ch 2, 2 dc) in next ch-2 sp, dc in next 7 sts, 2 dc in last st, turn. 18 dc, 1 (2 dc, ch 2, 2 dc) group

Row 4: Ch 3, dc in same st, (sk 1 st, dc in next st, dc in skipped st) 5 times, (2 dc, ch 2, 2 dc) in next ch-2 sp, (sk 1 st, dc in next st, dc in skipped st) 5 times, 2 dc in last st, turn. 24 dc, 1 (2 dc, ch 2, 2 dc) group

Row 5: Ch 3, dc in same st, dc in next 13 sts, (2 dc, ch 2, 2 dc) in next ch-2 sp, dc in next 13 sts, 2 dc in last st, turn. 30 dc, 1 (2 dc, ch 2, 2 dc) group

Row 6: Ch 3, dc in same st, dc in next 16 sts, (2 dc, ch 2, 2 dc) in next ch-2 sp, dc in next 16 sts, 2 dc in last st, turn. 36 dc, 1 (2 dc, ch 2, 2 dc) group

Row 7: Ch 3, dc in same st, (sk 1 st, dc in next st, dc in skipped st) 9 times, dc in next st, (2 dc, ch 2, 2 dc) in next ch-2 sp, dc in next st, (sk 1 st, dc in next st, dc in skipped st) 9 times, 2 dc in last st, turn. 42 dc, 1 (2 dc, ch 2, 2 dc) group

Row 8: Ch 3, dc in same st, dc in next 22 sts, (2 dc, ch 2, 2 dc) in next ch-2 sp, dc in next 22 sts, 2 dc in last st, turn. 48 dc, 1 (2 dc, ch 2, 2 dc) group

Row 9: Ch 3, dc in same st, dc in next 25 sts, (2 dc, ch 2, 2 dc) in next ch-2 sp, dc in next 25 sts, 2 dc in last st, turn. 54 dc, 1 (2 dc, ch 2, 2 dc) group

Row 10: Ch 3, dc in same ch-3 st, (sk 1 st, dc in next st, dc in skipped st) 14 times, (2 dc, ch 2, 2 dc) in next ch-2 sp, (sk 1 st, dc in next st, dc in skipped st) 14 times, 2 dc in last st, turn. 60 dc, 1 (2 dc, ch 2, 2 dc) group. Do not fasten off.

Tie and Trim

Rnd 1: Cont from Row 9, ch 35 (first tie), sc in 2nd ch from hook and in each ch across, sc evenly across ends of rows on top of bib, ch 35 (second tie), sc in 2nd ch from hook and in each ch across, working across next side, sc in next st, (ch 3, sk 1 st, sc in next st) 15 times, ch 3, sc in ch-2 sp, ch 3, sc in next st, (ch 3, sk 1 st, sc in next st) 15 times, sc in next st; join with sl st to st on edge of corner.
Fasten off. Weave in ends.

SHORTS

Yarn
Premier Yarns Cotton Sprout; light weight #3; 100% cotton; 3.5 oz (100 g) / 230 yd (210 m) per ball
- 1149-20 Cadet, 1 ball

Hook and Other Materials
- US size 7 (4.5 mm) crochet hook
- Yarn needle

Finished Measurements
3–6 Months (6–9 Months, 9–12 Months)
Waist: 13½ (15, 16½) in / 34.4 (38.2, 42) cm

Gauge
16 sc x 20 rows = 4 in (10.2 cm)

INSTRUCTIONS

Waistband
Ch 9 (13, 13).
Row 1: Sc in 2nd ch from hook and in each ch across, turn. 8 (12, 12) sc.
Rows 2–60 (66, 70): Ch 1, working in the BLO (see Stitch Guide, page 98), sc in each st across, turn.

Body, Part 1
Row 1: Ch 1, working along ends of rows, sc in next 30 (33, 35) sts, leaving the rem unworked, turn. 30 (33, 35) sc.
Rows 2–20 (24, 26): Ch 1, sc in each st across, turn.

Decrease

Rows 21–28 (25–32, 27–34): Ch 1, sc in next st, sc2tog, sc in each st across to last 3 sts, sc2tog, sc in last st, turn. 2 sts decreased per row ending with 14 (17, 19) sc.

Middle

Rows 29–38 (33–42, 35–44): Ch 1, sc in each st across, turn. 14 (17, 19) sc

Increase

Rows 39–46 (43–50, 45–52): Ch 1, 2 sc in first st, sc in each st across to last, 2 sc in last st, turn. 2 sts increased per row ending with 30 (33, 35) sc.

Body, Part 2

To complete Shorts, "ch 1, sc in each st across, turn" for 20 (24, 26) rows. 30 (33, 35) sc

Sew Body, Part 2 to Waistband. Sew sides of Body together, leaving Decrease, Middle, and Increase sections open for Leg.

Leg Opening Trim

All sizes:

Rnd 1: Join at bottom Middle, ch 1, using ends of rows as sts, sc in each st around, join with sl st to first sc.

Rnds 2 and 3: Ch 1, sc in each st around, join with sl st to first sc.

Rnds 4–6: Ch 1, working in BLO, sc in each st around, join with sl st to first sc.

Fasten off. Repeat on opposite side. Weave in ends.

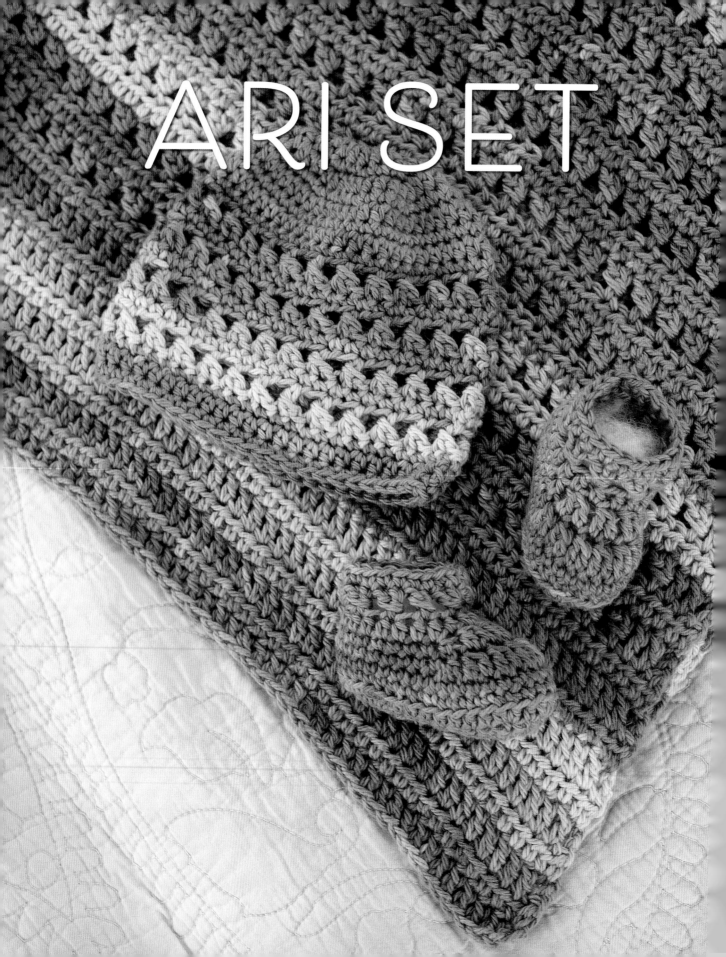

ARI SET

HAT, BOOTIES, BLANKET

Stay warm and cozy in this set! It's perfect for an afternoon out—or in!

HAT

Yarn
Premier Yarns Hipster Cotton; light weight #3; cotton; 3.5 oz (100 g) / 229 yd (210 m) per ball
• 2010-13 Canyon Walls, 1 ball

Hook and Other Materials
• US size G-6 (4 mm) crochet hook
• Yarn needle

Gauge
20 sc x 24 rows = 4 in (10.2 cm)

Finished Measurements
Newborn (3–6 Months, 9–12 Months)
Circumference: 14 (16, 18) in / 35.7 (40.7, 45.8) cm
Height: 5 (5¾, 6½) in / 12.7 (14.76, 16.5) cm

Pattern Note
• Do not start each new round with a chain stitch. Join rounds by working continuously into each new round.

INSTRUCTIONS
Create a magic ring (see Stitch Guide, page 94).

Rnd 1: 10 sc in ring. (10 sc)

Rnd 2: 2 hdc in each st around. (20 hdc)

Rnd 3: *Sc in next st, 2 sc in next st; rep from * around. (30 sc)

Rnd 4: *Hdc in next 2 sts, 2 hdc in next st; rep from * around. (40 hdc)

Rnd 5: *Sc in next 3 sts, 2 sc in next st; rep from* around. (50 sc)

Size Newborn only:

Rnd 6: Hdc in each st around.

Rnd 7: Sc in each st around.

Rnd 8: Rep Rnd 6.

Rnd 9: Rep Rnd 7, join with sl st to first first st.

Rnd 10: Ch 2 (this ch-2 is not considered a stitch), dc in same st, dc around ch-2 and dc, sk 1 st, *dc in next st, fpdc around dc (see Stitch Guide, page 108), sk 1 st; rep from * around, join with sl st to first dc.

Rnd 11: Ch 1, sc in each st around, join with sl st to first sc.

Rnds 12–17: Rep Rnds 10 and 11.

Rnd 18: Ch 2, hdc in each st around, join with sl st to first hdc.

Rnd 19: Ch 1, sc in each st around, join with sl st to first sc.

Fasten off. Weave in ends.

Size 3–6 Months only:

Rnd 6: *Hdc in next 4 sts, 2 hdc in next st; rep from * around. (60 hdc)

Rnd 7: Sc in each st around.

Rnd 8: Hdc in each st around.

Rnds 9–12: Rep Rnds 7 and 8. After Rnd 12 is complete, sl st to first hdc of rnd to join.

Rnd 13: Ch 2 (this ch-2 is not considered a stitch), dc in same st, dc around ch-2 and dc, sk 1 st, *dc in next st, fpdc on dc post just made (see Stitch Guide, page 108), sk 1 st; rep from * around, join with sl st to first dc.

Rnd 14: Ch 1, sc in each st around, join with sl st to first sc.

Rnds 15–20: Rep Rnds 13 and 14.

Rnd 21: Ch 2, hdc in each st around, join with sl st to first hdc.

Rnd 22: Ch 1, sc in each st around, join with sl st to first sc.

Fasten off. Weave in ends.

Size 9–12 Months only:

Rnd 6: *Hdc in next 4 sts, 2 hdc in next st; rep from * around. (60 hdc)

Rnd 7: *Sc in next 5 sts, 2 hdc in next st; rep from * around. (70 sc)

Rnd 8: Hdc in each st around.

Rnd 9: Sc in each st around.

Rnds 10–13: Rep Rnds 8 and 9. After Rnd 13 is complete, join with sl st to first st.

Rnd 14: Ch 2 (this ch-2 is not considered a stitch), dc in same st, fpdc around ch-2 and dc, sk 1 st, *dc in next st, fpdc around dc post just made (see Stitch Guide, page 108), sk 1 st; rep from * around, join with sl st to first dc.

Rnd 15: Ch 1, sc in each st around, join with sl st to first sc.

Rnds 16–21: Rep Rnds 14 and 15.

Rnd 22: Ch 2, hdc in each st around, join with sl st to first hdc.

Rnd 23: Ch 1, sc in each st around, join with sl st to first sc.

Fasten off. Weave in ends.

BOOTIES

Yarn
Premier Yarns Hipster Cotton; light weight #3; cotton; 3.5 oz (100 g) / 229 yd (210 m) per ball
- 2010-13 Canyon Walls, 1 ball

Hook and Other Materials
- US size G-6 (4 mm) crochet hook
- Yarn needle

Finished Measurements
3–6 Months (9–12 Months)
Width: 2 (2) in / 5.1 (5.1) cm
Height: 3 (3½) in / 7.7 (9) cm

Gauge
20 sc x 24 rows = 4 in (10.2 cm)

INSTRUCTIONS

Size 3–6 Months:

Sole
Ch 8.

Rnd 1: Sc in second ch from hook and in each ch across to last ch, 4 hdc in last ch, working in free loops of beginning ch, sc in next 5 chs, 3 sc in next ch, join with sl st to first sc. (18 sts)

Rnd 2: Ch 1, sc in same st as joining st and in next 3 sts, hdc in next 2 sts, 2 dc in each of next 4 sts, hdc in next 2 sts, sc in next 3 sts, 2 sc in each of last 3 sts, join with sl st to first sc. (25 sts)

Rnd 3: Ch 2 (this ch-2 is not considered a stitch), hdc in same st as joining st and in next 6 sts, 2 hdc in next st, (hdc in next st, 2 hdc in next st) 3 times, hdc in next 5 sts, (sc in next sc, 2 sc in next st) 3 times, join with sl st to first hdc. (32 sts)

Boot

Rnd 4: Ch 1, working in BLO (see Stitch Guide, page 98), sc in each st around, join with sl st to the first sc.

Rnd 5: Ch 1, sc in each st around, join with sl st to the first sc.

Rnd 6: Ch 1, sc in same st as joining st and in next 3 sts, sc2tog, hdc2tog, (dc2tog) 6 times, hdc2tog, sc2tog, sc in each st to end, join with sl st to first sc. (22 sts)

Rnd 7: Ch 1, sc in same st as joining and in next 3 sts, hdc2tog, (dc2tog) 3 times, hdc2tog, sc in each st to end, join with sl st to first sc. (17 sts)

Rnd 8: Ch 2, hdc in each st around to last 2 sts, hdc2tog, join with sl st to first hdc. (16 hdc)

Cuff

Rnd 9: Ch 2, dc in same ch-2 st, fpdc on dc post just made (see Stitch Guide, page 108), sk 1 st, *dc in next st, dc around dc post just made, sk 1 st; rep from * around, join with sl st to first first dc.

Rnd 10: Ch 1, sc in each st around, join with sl st to first sc.

Fasten off. Weave in ends.

Size 9–12 Months:

Sole

Ch 10.

Rnd 1: Sc in second ch from hook and in each ch across to last ch, 4 hdc in last ch, working in free loops of beginning ch, sc in next 7 chs, 3 sc in next ch, join with sl st to first sc. (22 sts)

Rnd 2: Ch 1, sc in same st as joining st and in next 5 sts, hdc in next 2 sts, 2 dc in each of next 4 sts, hdc in next 2 sts, sc in next 5 sts, 2 sc in each of last 3 sts, join with sl st to first sc. (29 sts)

Rnd 3: Ch 2 (this ch-2 is not considered a stitch), hdc in same st as joining st and in next 8 sts, 2 hdc in next st, (hdc in next st, 2 hdc in next st) 3 times, hdc in next 7 sts, (sc in next sc, 2 sc in next st) 3 times, join with sl st to first hdc. (36 sts)

Boot

Rnd 4: Ch 1, working in BLO (see Stitch Guide, page 98), sc in each st around, join with sl st to the first sc.

Rnd 5: Ch 1, sc in each st around, join with sl st to the first sc.

Rnd 6: Ch 1, sc in same st as joining st and in next 5 sts, sc2tog, hdc2tog, (dc2tog) 6 times, hdc2tog, sc2tog, sc in each st to end, join with sl st to first sc. (26 sts)

Rnd 7: Ch 1, sc in same st as joining st and in next 5 sts, hdc2tog, (dc2tog) 3 times, hdc2tog, sc in each st to end, join with sl st to first sc. (21 sts)

Rnd 8: Ch 2 (this ch-2 is not considered a stitch), hdc in each st around to last 2 sts, hdc2tog, join with sl st to first hdc. (20 hdc)

Cuff

Rnd 9: Ch 2, dc in same st, fpdc on dc post just made (see Stitch Guide, page 108), sk 1 st, *dc in next st, fpdc on dc post just made, sk 1 st; rep from * around, join with sl st to first first dc.

Rnd 10: Ch 1, sc in each st around, join with sl st to first st.

Fasten off. Weave in ends.

BLANKET

Yarn
Premier Yarns Hipster Cotton; light weight #3; cotton; 3.5 oz (100 g) / 229 yd (210 m) per ball
- 2010-13 Canyon Walls, 1 ball

Hook and Other Materials
- US size H-8 (5 mm) crochet hook
- Yarn needle

Finished Measurements
Length: 31 in (78.8 cm)
Width: 33 in (84cm)

Gauge
14 dc x 11 rows = 4 in (10.2 cm) in pattern

INSTRUCTIONS
Ch 120.

Beginning Border
Row 1: Dc in 4th ch from hook and in each ch across, turn. (118 dc)
Row 2: Ch 1, hdc in each st across, turn.
Row 3: Ch 3 (counts as dc), dc in each st across, turn.
Rep Rows 2 and 3 until Beginning Border measures 4 in (10.2 cm).

Middle
Row 1: Ch 3, dc in next 2 sts, *dc in next st, fpdc around dc post just made (see Stitch Guide, page 108), sk 1 st; rep from * across to last 3 sts, dc in last 3 sts, turn.
Row 2: Ch 2, hdc in each st across, turn.
Rep Rows 1 and 2 of Middle until Blanket measures 23 in (58.4 cm).

Ending Border
Rep Rows 2 and 3 of Beginning Border until Ending Border measures 4 in (10.2 cm).
Fasten off. Weave in ends.

CHLOE
SET

SWEATER, LEGGINGS, HAT

Easy to make and oh-so-cute to wear! This sweater is perfect for any weather. The lightweight style is sweet and not too hot. The leggings, well, you can't beat them, and the hat is just the perfect touch!

SWEATER

Yarn
Premier Yarns Bloom DK; light weight #3; 100% acrylic; 7 oz (200 g) / 656 yd (600 m) per skein
- 1090-15 Gerbera, 1 skein

Hook and Other Materials
- US size G-6 (4 mm) crochet hook
- Yarn needle

Finished Measurements
Sizes 3–6 Months (6–12 Months)
To fit chest: 17 (18) in / 43.3 (45.8) cm
Finished Chest: 18½ (20) in / 47.2 (51.8) cm
Finished Length: 11 (12) in / 28 (30.6) cm

Gauge
20 sts x 20 rows = 4 in (10.2 cm) in pattern

INSTRUCTIONS

Size 3–6 Months (6–12 Months):

Front
Ch 39 (41).
Row 1 (WS): Sc in second ch from hook and in each across, turn. 38 (40) sc
Row 2: Ch 2, hdc in each st across, turn.
Row 3: Ch 1, sc in each st across, turn.
Row 4: Ch 2, hdc in each st across, turn.

Rep Rep Rows 3 and 4 until panel measures 6 (6½) in / 15.3 (16.6) cm.
Fasten off.

Sleeves
Row 1: Ch 32 (34), sc in each st across main panel, ch 33 (35), turn. 65 (69) chs, 38 (40) sc
Row 2: Hdc in 2nd ch from hook and in each ch across, hdc in each st across, hdc in each ch across. 102 (108) hdc
Row 3: Ch 1, sc in each st across, turn.
Row 4: Ch 1, hdc in each st across, turn.
Rep Rows 3 and 4 for 3¾ (4) in / 9.6 (10.2) cm, ending on Row 3.

Head Opening
Row 1: Ch 2, hdc in next 31 (33) sts, ch 76, sk 76 sts, sc in next 42 (43) sts, turn.
Row 2: Ch 2, hdc in each st and ch across, turn. 102 (108) hdc
Rep Rows 3 and 4 of Sleeves for 3¾ (4) in / 9.6 (10.2) cm, ending on Row 3.
Fasten off.

Back
Row 1: Skip 31 (33) sts and join in next st, ch 2, hdc in next 38 (40) sts, turn.
Row 2: Ch 1, sc in each st across, turn.
Row 3: Ch 2, hdc in each st across, turn.
Rep Rows 2 and 3 until Back measures 6 (6½) in / 15.3 (16.6) cm.
Fasten off.

Assembly
Fold panel in half at Head Opening with RS facing. Sew under arm and down body. Rep on opposite side.

Bottom Trim
Rnd 1: Join yarn at seam, ch 2 (this ch-2 is not considered a stitch), hdc in each st around, join with sl st in first hdc.

Rnds 2–4: Ch 2, working in the 3rd lp of hdc (see Stitch Guide, page 101), hdc in each st around, join with sl st in first hdc.
Fasten off.

Sleeve Trim
Rnd 1: Join at seam, ch 2 (this ch 2 is not considered a st), use ends of rows as stitches, hdc in each st around, join with sl st in first hdc.

Rnds 2–4: Working in the 3rd lp of hdc, hdc in each st around, join.
Fasten off. Weave in ends

HAT

Yarn

Premier Yarns Bloom DK; light weight #3; 100% acrylic; 7 oz (200 g) / 656 yd (600 m) per skein
- 1090-15 Gerbera, 1 skein

Hook and Other Materials
- US size G-6 (4 mm) crochet hook
- Yarn needle

Finished Measurements

Newborn (3–6 Months, 9–12 Months)
Circumference: 14 (16, 18) in / 35.7 (40.7, 45.8) cm
Height: 5½ (6¼, 7) in / 14 (15.9, 17.8) cm

Gauge

18 dc x 12 rows = 4 in (10.2 cm) in pattern

INSTRUCTIONS

Ch 61 (73, 81).

Rnd 1: Hdc in 2nd ch from hook and in each ch across, join with sl st to first hdc. 60, (72, 80) hdc

Rnds 2–4: Ch 2 (this ch-2 is not considered a stitch here and throughout), working in 3rd lp of hdc (see Stitch Guide, page 101), hdc in each st around, join with sl st to first hdc.

Rnd 5: Ch 2, *dc in next 2 sts, tr in next 2 sts; rep from * around, join with sl st to first dc.

Rnd 6: Ch 5 (this stitch counts as a double crochet and a ch-2 here and throughout), sk next st, *dc in next 2, ch 2, sk 2 sts; rep from * around, join with sl st to ch-3 of beg ch-5

Rnd 7: Ch 2, *dc in next 2 sts, 2 dc in next ch-2 sp; rep from * around, join with sl st to first dc.

Rnds 8 and 9: Rep Rnds 6 and 7.

Rnd 10: Ch 2, dc in each st around, join with sl st to first dc.

Rep Rnd 10 until Hat measures 5 (5¾, 6½) in / 12.7 (14.7, 16.5) cm.

Crown Decrease

Size Newborn only:

Rnd 1: Ch 2 (this ch-2 is not considered a stitch here and throughout), *dc in next 4 sts, dc2tog; rep from * around, join with sl st to first dc. (50 dc)

Rnd 2: Ch 2, *dc in next 3 sts, dc2tog; rep from * around, join with sl st to first dc. (40 dc)

Rnd 3: Ch 2, *dc in next 2 sts, dc2tog; rep from * around, join with sl st to first dc. (30 dc)

Rnd 4: Ch 2, *dc in next st, dc2tog; rep from * around, join with sl st to first dc. (20 dc)

Rnd 5: Ch 2, (dc2tog) 10 times; join with sl st to first dc. (10 dc)

Fasten off leaving a long tail for sewing. Thread tapestry needle with long end and close last rnd.

Size 3–6 Months only:

Rnd 1: Ch 2 (this ch-2 is not considered a stitch here and throughout), *dc in next 4 sts, dc2tog; rep from * around, join with sl st to first dc. (60 dc)

Rnd 2: Ch 2, *dc in next 3 sts, dc2tog; rep from * around, join with sl st to first dc. (48 dc)

Rnd 3: Ch 2, *dc in next 2 sts, dc2tog; rep from * around, join with sl st to first dc. (36 dc)

Rnd 4: Ch 2, *dc in next st, dc2tog; rep from * around, join with sl st to first dc. (24 dc)

Rnd 5: Ch 2, (dc2tog) 12 times; join with sl st to first dc. (12 dc)

Fasten off leaving a long tail for sewing. Thread tapestry needle with long end and close last rnd.

Size 9–12 Months only:

Rnd 1: Ch 2 (this ch-2 is not considered a stitch here and throughout), *dc in next 2 sts, dc2tog; rep from * around, join with sl st to first dc. (60 dc)

Rnd 2: Ch 2, *dc in next 4 sts, dc2tog; rep from * around, join with sl st to first dc. (50 dc)

Rnd 3: Ch 2, *dc in next 3 sts, dc2tog; rep from * around, join with sl st to first dc. (40 dc)

Rnd 4: Ch 2, *dc in next 2 sts, dc2tog; rep from * around, join with sl st to first dc. (30 dc)

Rnd 5: Ch 2, *dc in next st, dc2tog; rep from * around, join with sl st to first dc. (20 dc)

Rnd 6: Ch 2, (dc2tog) 10 times; join with sl st to first dc. (10 dc)

Fasten off leaving a long tail for sewing. Thread tapestry needle with long end and close last rnd.

Finishing

Create a large pom-pom and tie to top of Hat.
Weave in ends.

LEGGINGS

Yarn

Premier Yarns Bloom DK; light weight #3; 100% acrylic; 7 oz (200 g) / 656 yd (600 m) per skein
- 1090-15 Gerbera, 1 skein

Hook and Other Materials

US size 7 (4.5 mm) crochet hook
Yarn needle

Finished Measurements

3–6 Months (9–12 Months)
Width: 3 (3½) in / 7.7 (8.8) cm
Length: 7½ (8) in / 19.1 (20.4) cm

Gauge

18 dc x 9 rows = 4 in (10.2 cm)

INSTRUCTIONS

Ch 25 (29).

Rnd 1: Hdc in 2nd ch from hook and in each ch across, join with sl st to first hdc. 24 (28) hdc

Rnds 2-4: Ch 2 (this ch-2 is not considered a stitch here and throughout), working in the 3rd lp of hdc (see Stitch Guide, page 101), hdc in each st around, join with sl st to first hdc.

Rnd 5: Ch 3 (this stitch counts as a double crochet), dc in each st around, join with sl st to first dc.

Rnd 6: Ch 2, *dc in next 2 sts, ch 2, sk 2 sts; rep from * around, join with sl to first dc.

Rnd 7: Ch 2, *dc in next 2 sts, 2 dc in next ch-2 sp; rep from * around, join with sl st to first dc.

Rnds 8 and 9: Rep Rnds 6 and 7.

Rnds 10-14 (16): Rep Rnd 5.

Rnds 15-18 (17-20): Rep Rnds 6 and 7.

Rnd 19 (21): Ch 2, hdc in each st around, join with sl st to first hdc.

Rnds 20-22 (22-24): Ch 2, working in the 3rd lp of hdc, hdc in each st around, join with sl st to first hdc.

Fasten off.

EVIE SET

HEADBAND, SANDALS, DRESS

Jazz up any gift with this dress set. It's sweet and dainty, yet the accessories add the precious touch! The sandals can be worn anytime as well as the headband, so mix and match them with any set, too.

HEADBAND

Yarn
Premier Yarns Cotton Sprout; light weight #3; 100% cotton; 3.5 oz (100 g) / 230 yd (210 m) per ball
- A: 1149-01 Cranberry, 1 ball
- B: 1149-06 Blush, 1 ball
- C: 1149-30 Silver, 1 ball

Hook and Other Materials
- US size D-3 (3.25mm) crochet hook
- Yarn needle

Finished Measurements
Newborn (3–6 Months, 9–12 Months)
Circumference: 14 (16, 18) in / 35.7 (40.7, 45.8) cm

Gauge
25 sts x 16 rows = 4 in (10.2 cm) in pattern

INSTRUCTIONS
With A, ch 12.
Row 1: Hdc in 2nd ch from hook and in each ch across, turn. (11 hdc)
Row 2: Ch 1, working in BLO (see Stitch Guide, page 98), sc in each st across, turn.

Row 3: Ch 2, working in FLO (see Stitch Guide, page 98), hdc in each st across, turn.
Rep Rows 2 and 3 until headband measures 14 (16, 18) in / 35.7 (40.7, 45.8) cm.

Trim
Rnd 1: Sl st across last rnd, ch 1, sl st across ends of rows, ch 1, sl st across foundation ch row, ch 1, sl st across, join with sl st to first sl st.
Fasten off, leaving a long tail for sewing.

Assembly
Thread yarn needle with long tail and sew the short ends together.
Pinch the seam and sew in place.

Flower
With B, ch 40.
Rnd 1: Tr in 4th ch from hook, *ch 2, tr in next st; rep from * across.
Fasten off, leaving a long tail for sewing.
Roll strip into a spiral flower and use yarn needle to sew together.

Flower Center
With C, create a magic ring (see Stitch Guide, page 94).
Rnd 1: 6 sc in ring, join with sl st to first sc. (6 sc)
Fasten off leaving a long tail for sewing.

Finishing
Sew Flower Center in center of Flower.
Sew Flower on pinched seam.
Weave in ends.

SANDALS

Yarn
Premier Yarns Cotton Sprout; light weight #3; 100% cotton; 3.5 oz (100 g) / 230 yd (210 m) per ball
- A: 1149-01 Cranberry, 1 ball
- B: 1149-06 Blush, 1 ball
- C: 1149-30 Silver, 1 ball

Hook and Other Materials
- US size D-3 (3.25 mm) crochet hook
- Yarn needle

Finished Measurements
3–6 Months (9–12 Months)
Width: 2 (2) in / 5.1 (5.1) cm)
Height: 3 (3½) in / 7.7 (9) cm

Gauge
20 sc x 20 rows = 4 in (10.2 cm)

INSTRUCTIONS

Sole
Make 2 in color A and 2 in color C.

Size 3–6 Months:
With A, ch 8.
Rnd 1: Sc in second ch from hook and in each ch across to last ch, 4 hdc in last ch, working in free loops of beginning ch, sc in next 5 chs, 3 sc in next ch, join with sl st to first sc. (18 sts)
Rnd 2: Ch1, sc in same st as joining st and in next 3 sts, hdc in next 2 sts, 2 dc in each of next 4 sts, hdc in next 2 sts, sc in next 3 sts, 2 sc in each of last 3 sts, join with sl st to first sc. (25 sts)
Rnd 3: Ch 2 (this ch-2 is not considered a stitch), hdc in same st as joining st and in next 6 sts, 2 hdc in next st, (hdc in next st, 2 hdc in next st) 3 times, hdc in next 5 sts, place marker in hdc just made, (sc in next sc, 2 sc in next st) 3 times, join with sl st to first hdc. (32 sts)

Size 9–12 Months:
With A, ch 10.
Rnd 1: Sc in second ch from hook and in each ch across to last ch, 4 hdc in last ch, working in free loops of beginning ch, sc in next 7 chs, 3 sc in next ch, join with sl st to first sc. (22 sts)
Rnd 2: Ch1, sc in same st as joining st and in next 5 sts, hdc in next 2 sts, 2 dc in each of next 4 sts, hdc in next 2 sts, sc in next 5 sts, 2 sc in each of last 3 sts, join with sl st to first sc. (29 sts)
Rnd 3: Ch 2 (this ch-2 is not considered a stitch), hdc in same st as joining st and in next 8 sts, 2 hdc in next st, (hdc in next st, 2 hdc in next st) 3 times, hdc in next 7 sts, place marker in hdc just made, (sc in next sc, 2 sc in next st) 3 times, join with sl st to first hdc. (36 sts)

Assembly

All sizes:

Rnd 1: Place WS of Sole color A and Sole color C together. With Sole color C facing up and working with Sole color A, sl st around each st, join with sl st to first st.

Fasten off.

Body

Size 3–6 Months:

Rnd 1: Join color A in 10th st from marked st around heel on Rnd 3 of Sole. Ch 1, working in BLO of sl st (see Stitch Guide, page 98), sc in each st around, join with sl st to the first sc. (32 sc)

Rnd 2: Ch 1, sc in next 7 sts, hdc in next 12 sts, sc in each st around, join with sl st to first sc.

Rnd 3: Ch 1, sc in same st as joining st and in next 4 sts, sc2tog, dc2tog 4 times, sc2tog, sc in next 4 sts, (sc in next st, sc2tog) 3 times, join with sl st to first sc. (21 sts)

Rnd 4: Ch 1, sc in same st as joining st and in next 3 sts, hdc2tog, dc2tog 2 times, hdc2tog, sc in each st to end, join with sl st to first sc. (17 sts)

Rnd 5: Ch 1, sc in next 4 sts, ch 6 (strap), sl st in 2nd ch from hook and in next 4 chs, sc in next unworked st, sc in each st until 5 sts remain, dc in last 5 sts, join with sl st to first sc.

Fasten off. Weave in ends.

Size 9–12 Months:

Rnd 1: Join color A in 10th st from marked st around heel on Rnd 3 of Sole. Ch 1, working in BLO of sl st (see Stitch Guide, page 98), sc in each st around, join with sl st to the first sc. (36 sc)

Rnd 2: Ch 1, sc in next 7 sts, hdc in next 12 sts, sc in each st around, join with sl st to first sc.

Rnd 3: Ch 1, sc in same st as joining st and in next 5 sts, sc2tog, (dc2tog 6) times, sc2tog, sc in next 5 sts 3 times, join with sl st to first sc. (25 sts)

Rnd 4: Ch 1, sc in same st as joining st and in next 4 sts, hdc2tog, (dc2tog 3) times, hdc2tog, sc in each st to end, join with sl st to first sc. (20 sts)

Rnd 5: Ch 1, sc in next 4 sts, ch 6 (strap), sl st in 2nd ch from hook and in next 4 chs, sc in next unworked st, sc in each st until 5 sts remain, dc in last 5 sts, join with sl st to first sc.

Fasten off. Weave in ends.

Flower

With B, ch 25.

Rnd 1: Tr in 4th ch from hook, *ch 2, tr in next st; rep from * across.

Fasten off leaving a long tail for sewing.

Roll strip into a spiral flower and use yarn needle to sew together.

DRESS

Yarn

Premier Yarns Cotton Sprout; light weight #3; 100% cotton; 3.5 oz (100 g) / 230 yd (210 m) per ball

- A: 1149-01 Cranberry, 1 ball
- B: 1149-06 Blush, 1 ball
- C: 1149-30 Silver, 1 ball

Hook and Other Materials

- US size 7 (4.5 mm) crochet hook
- Yarn needle

Finished Measurements

3–6 Months (6–12 Months)
Chest: 16 (17) in / 40.7 (43.3) cm
Length: 10 (12) in / 25.5 (30.5) cm

Gauge

16 dc x 10 rows = 4 in (10.2 cm)

INSTRUCTIONS

Yoke

With color A, ch 51 (56).

Row 1 (RS): Hdc in 2nd ch from hook and in each ch across, turn. 50 (55) hdc

Row 2: *Hdc in next 9 (10) sts, 2 hdc in next st; rep from * across, turn. 55 (60) hdc

Fasten off, join C.

Row 3: *Sc in next 10 (11) sts, 2 sc in next st; rep from * across, turn. 60 (65) sc

Row 4: *Sc in next 11 (12) sts, 2 sc in next st; rep from * across, turn. 65 (70) sc

Fasten off. Join with color A.

Row 5: *Hdc in next 12 (13) sts, 2 hdc in next st; rep from * across, turn. 70 (75) hdc

Row 6: *Hdc in next 13 (14) sts, 2 hdc in next st; rep from * across, turn. 75 (80) hdc

Row 7: *Hdc in next 14 (15) sts, 2 hdc in next st; rep from * across, turn. 80 (85) hdc

Row 8: *Hdc in next 15 (16) sts, 2 hdc in next st; rep from * across, turn. 85 (90) hdc

Fasten off leaving a long tail for sewing. Thread tapestry needle and sew short ends together.

Body

All sizes:

Rnd 1 (RS): With RS facing, join color A in first st by seam, ch 2 (this ch-2 is not considered a stitch), dc in next 14 (15) sts to the right of seam (creating half of Back first), ch 11, sk 14 (15) sts, dc in next 28 (30) sts, ch 11, sk next 14 (15) sts, dc in next 14 (15 sts), join with sl st to first dc (not ch-2). 56 (60) dc and 2 ch-11 sps

Rnd 2: Ch 2, dc in next 14 (15) sts, 11 dc in ch-11 sp, dc in next 28 (30) sts, 11 dc in next ch-11 sp, dc in next 14 (15) sts, join with sl st to first dc. 78 (82) dc

Size 3–6 Months only:

Rnd 3: Ch 2, dc in next 12 sts, 2 dc in next st; rep from * around, join with sl st to first dc. (84 dc)

Rnds 4–6: Ch 2, dc in each st around.

Rnd 7: Ch 2, dc in each st around, join with sl st to first dc.

Rep Rnd 7 until Dress measures 8¼ in (21 cm).

Fasten off.

Size 6–12 Months only:

Rnd 3: Ch 2, dc in next 4 sts, *dc in next 12 sts, 2 dc in next st; rep from * around, join with sl st to first dc. (88 dc)

Rnds 4–6: Ch 2, dc in each st around.

Rnd 7: Ch 2, dc in next 4 sts, *dc in next 13 sts, 2 dc in next st; rep from * around, join with sl st to first dc. (94 dc)

Rnd 8: Ch 2, dc in each st around.

Rep Rnd 8 until Dress measures 8¾ in (22.4 cm).

Fasten off.

All sizes:

Rnd 1 (RS): Join color C, ch 1, sc in each st around, join with sl st to first st, TURN.

Rnd 2 (WS): Ch 1, sc in each st around, join with sl st to first sc, TURN.

Fasten off.

Rnd 3: Join color A, ch 1, sc in each st around, join with sl st to first sc.

Fasten off.

Rnd 4: Join color A with sl st, sk 1 st, 3 dc in next st, sk 1 st, *sl st in next st, sk 1 st, 3 dc in next st, sk 1 st; rep from * around until 2 sts remain, 3dc in next st, join with sl st to first dc. This round may not work out exactly, but it won't be noticeable in the piece.

Fasten off.

Flower

With B, ch 40.

Rnd 1: Tr in 4th ch from hook, *ch 2, tr in next st; rep from * across.

Fasten off leaving a long tail for sewing. Roll strip into a spiral flower and use yarn needle to sew together. Use photo as a guide to sew flower on Dress. Weave in ends.

RORY
SET

SOCKS, VEST, BLANKET

Try your hand at a sweet sock set, a vest, and a matching blanket. Subtle details add the perfect touch and style.

SOCKS

Yarn
Premier Yarns Bamboo Fair; light weight #3; 60% bamboo, 40% cotton; 3.5 oz (100 g) / 273 yd (250 m) per ball
- A: 1107-36 Harvest, 1 ball

Hook and Other Materials
- US size C-2 (2.75 mm) crochet hook
- Yarn needle

Finished Measurements
Toe to back of heel:
3–6 Months: 3½ in / (9 cm)
9–12 Months: 4 in / (10.2 cm)

Gauge
16 sc x 16 rows = 4 in (10.2 cm)

Pattern Notes
- The socks are crocheted from the toe to the cuff.

INSTRUCTIONS

Size 3–6 Months:

Toe/Foot
Do not start each new round with a chain stitch. Join rounds by working continuously into each new round. Ch 2.
Rnd 1: 8 sc in second ch from hook, do not join. (8 sts)
Rnd 2: Working in rounds, 2 sc in each st. (16 sts)
Rnd 3: (Sc in next st, 2 sc in next st) around. (24 sts)
Rnd 4: (Sc in next 2 sts, 2 sc in next st) around. (32 sts)
Rnds 5–22: Sc in each st around.

Heel
Row 23: Sc in next 16 sts, leaving remaining sts unworked, turn. (16 sts)
Rows 24–28: Ch 1, sc in each st across, turn.
Row 29: Ch 1, sc in next 4 sts, sc2tog 4 times, sc in next 4 sts, turn. (12 sts)
Row 30: Ch 1, sc in next 4 sts, sc2tog 2 times, sc in next 4 sts. (10 sts)

Ankle
Rnd 31: Sl st to the first st of rnd, ch 1, using ends of rows as sts, sc 8, sc 16 across Foot, using ends of rows as sts, sc 8, join with sl st to first sc. (32 sts)
Rnd 32: Ch 1, sc in each st around, join with sl st to first sc. (32 sts)

Cuff

Rnd 33: Ch 4 (this stitch counts as the first dc and ch 1 here and throughout), sk 1 st, *dc in next st, ch 1, sk 1, rep from * around, join with sl st in ch-3 of beg ch-4.

Rnd 34: Ch 1, sc in each ch and st around, join with sl st to first sc.

Rnds 35 and 36: Rep Rnds 33 and 34.
Fasten off.

Finishing

Sew heel closed with yarn needle.
Weave in ends.

Size 9–12 Months:

Toe/Foot

Do not start each new round with a chain stitch. Join rounds by working continuously into each new round.

Ch 2.

Rnd 1: 8 sc in second ch from hook, do not join. (8 sts)

Rnd 2: Working in rnds continuosly, 2 sc in each st. (16 sts)

Rnd 3: (Sc in next st, 2 sc in next st) around. (24 sts)

Rnd 4: (Sc in next 2 sts, 2 sc in next st) around. (32 sts)

Rnd 5: (Sc in next 7 sts, 2 sc in next st around. (36 sts)

Rnds 6–26: Sc in each st around.

Heel

Row 27: Sc in next 18 sts, leaving remaining sts unworked, turn. (18 sts)

Rows 28–32: Ch 1, sc in each st across, turn.

Row 33: Ch 1, sc in next 5 sts, sc2tog 4 times, sc in next 5 sts, turn. (14 sts)

Row 34: Ch 1, sc in next 5 sts, sc2tog 2 times, sc in next 5 sts. (12 sts)

Ankle

Rnd 35: Sl st to the first st of rnd, ch 1, using ends of rows as sts, sc 8, sc 18 across Foot, using ends of rows as sts, sc 8, join with sl st to first sc. (34 sts)

Rnd 36: Ch 1, sc in each st around, join with sl st to first sc. (34 sts)

Cuff

Rnd 37: Ch 4 (this stitch counts as a first double crochet and a ch 1 here and throughout), sk 1 st, *dc in next st, ch 1, sk 1, rep from * around, join with sl st in ch-3 of beg ch-4.

Rnd 38: Ch 1, sc in each ch and st around, join with sl st in first sc.

Rnds 39 and 40: Rep Rnds 37 and 38.
Fasten off.

Finishing

Sew heel closed with yarn needle.
Weave in ends.

VEST

Yarn

Premier Yarns Bamboo Fair; light weight #3; 60% bamboo, 40% cotton; 3.5 oz (100 g) / 273 yd (250 m) per ball
• A: 1107-35 Moss, 2 balls

Hook and Other Materials
• US size G-6 (4 mm) crochet hook
• Yarn needle

Finished Measurements
3 Months (6 Months, 12 Months)
Chest: 18 (19, 20) in / 45.8 (48.4, 50.8) cm
Length: 9¼ (10, 10¾) in / 23.6 (25.5, 27.4) cm

Gauge
16 sc x 18 rows = 4 in (10.2 cm)

INSTRUCTIONS

Back

With A, ch 37 (41, 43).

Row 1: Sc in 2nd ch from hook and in each ch across, turn. 36 (40, 42) sc

Row 2: Ch 1, dc in each st across, turn.

Rep Row 2 until pieces measures 5 (5, 5¾) in/12.8 (12.8, 14.7) cm.

Shape Armholes

Row 1 (RS): Sl st in next 5 sts, ch 3 (this stitch counts as a double crochet here and throughout), dc in each across leaving last 5 sts unworked, turn. 26 (30, 32) sts

Row 2: Ch 3, dc in each st across, turn.

Rep Row 2 until piece measures 9¼ (10, 10¾) in / 23.6 (25.5, 27.4) cm.

Fasten off.

Front

Work same as Back through Row 2 of armhole shaping.

Left Front: Shape neck and shoulders

Next Row (RS): Ch 3, dc in next 12 (14, 15) sts, turn. 13, 15, 16 sts.

Rep last row until piece measures 9¼ (10, 10¾) in / 23.6 (25.5, 27.4) cm.

Right Front: Shape neck and shoulders

Pick up in next unworked st on Front on RS.

Next Row (RS): Ch 3, dc in next 12 (14, 15) sts, turn. 13 (15, 16) sts

Rep last row until piece measures 9¼ (10, 10¾) in / 23.6 (25.5, 27.4) cm.

Finishing

Lay pieces WS together and sew from bottom to armhole.

Sew shoulder seams.

Weave in ends.

Trim: Armholes and Neck Opening

Rnd 1: Join yarn in seam, ch 1, using ends of rows as sts, sc evenly around, join with sl st to first sc.

Fasten off.

BLANKET

Yarn
Premier Yarns Bamboo Fair; light weight
 #3; 60% bamboo, 40% cotton; 3.5 oz
 (100 g) / 273 yd (250 m) per ball
- A: 1107-35 Moss, 2 balls
- B: 1107-36 Harvest, 2 balls
- C: 1107-34 Thistle, 2 balls

Hook and Other Materials
- US size H-8 (5 mm) crochet hook
- Yarn needle

Finished Measurements
Height: 30 in (76.2 cm)
Width: 25 in (63.5 cm)

Gauge
16 dc x 12 rows = 4 in (10.2 cm)

Color Sequence
Change colors each row in the following
 order: A, B, C
Chain and Row 1: A
Row 2: B
Row 3: C
Continue to change colors each row in
 order of A, B, C.

*TIP: Leave long ends on each end of row
and, as you work the border, carry them
along the edge of the work to weave them
in.*

Pattern Note
- To change yarn color, work last stitch
 of old color to last yarn-over step. Yarn
 over with new color and draw through all
 loops on the hook to complete the stitch.
 Work over the strand of old color as you
 work each row. See also Stitch Guide,
 page 110.

INSTRUCTIONS

With A, ch 114.

Row 1: Sc in 2nd ch from hook and in each st across, turn. (113 sc) Fasten off, join next color.

Row 2: Ch 1, sc in first st, *ch 3, sk 3 sts, sc in next st; rep from * across, turn. Fasten off, join next color.

Row 3: Ch 3 (this stitch counts as a double crochet here and throughout), 4 dc in next ch-3 sp, *sk next st, 4 dc in next ch-3 sp; rep from * across to last st, dc in last st, turn. Fasten off, join next color.

Row 4: Ch 1, sc in first st, ch 3, sk 4 sts, *sc in sp between last skipped st and next st, ch 3, sk 4 sts; rep from * across, ending with sc in last st, turn. Fasten off, join next color.

Rep Rows 3 and 4 following Color Sequence until blanket measures 28 in (71.3 cm), ending on Rnd 4.

Last Row: Ch 1, sc in first st, *3 sc in next ch-3 sp, sc in next st; rep from * across, turn.

Border

Rnd 1: Join color B, ch 2 (this ch-2 is not considered a stitch), 2 hdc in same st, hdc in each st across to last st, 3 hdc in last st, hdc evenly across side, working along foundation ch, 3 hdc in first ch, hdc in each st across to last ch, 3 hdc in last ch, hdc evenly across next side, hdc in first st, join with sl st to first hdc.

Fasten off. Join with color C.

Rnd 2: Ch 2, hdc in each st around, working 3 hdc in each corner.

Fasten off C. Join with color A.

Rnd 3: Rep Rnd 2.

Fasten off. Weave in ends.

HOW TO READ THE PATTERNS

SYMBOLS AND TERMS

* **:** Work instructions following * as many times as indicated, in addition to the first time.

( ) **:** Work enclosed instructions as many times as specified by the number immediately following, or work all enclosed instructions in the stitch or space indicated, or contains explanatory remarks.

( ) at end of row or rnd: The number of stitches or spaces you should have after completing that row or round.

Gauge:

Exact gauge is essential for proper size of the finished garment. Before beginning your project, make the sample swatch given in the individual instructions with the yarn and hook specified. After completing the swatch, measure it, counting your stitches and rows carefully. If your swatch is larger or smaller than specified, make another swatch, changing the hook size to get the correct gauge. Keep trying until you find the size hook that will give you the specified gauge.

Materials:

Items you will need to complete the patterns in this book include crochet hooks, stitch markers, pins, scissors, yarn, ruler, a yarn needle, and other items as given in the list for each pattern.

- **Crochet hooks:** Each pattern will list the crochet hook needed for that project. Always start with the hook size stated and check the gauge before starting the project. Change the hook size as necessary to obtain the correct gauge so that the project will be finished in the correct size.
- **Stitch markers:** Stitch markers are used to mark specific stitches in a pattern. If you do not have access to ready-made markers, use a piece of scrap yarn or even a bobby pin to mark the stitch.
- **Yarn needle:** The yarn needle is a large needle with a big eye suitable for yarn, used to sew different pieces together and for weaving in ends.

Yarn:

You will find, listed within each pattern, the specific yarn(s) and colors I used to crochet the items, plus how many skeins you'll need. Also included is that specific yarn's "yarn weight." You'll find this information on the label of every skein of yarn you buy, and it ranges from #0 (lace weight) to #7 (jumbo weight). If you can't find the specific yarn I use or you'd like to use something else, knowing the yarn weight will help you pick another yarn that will have the same gauge.

Standard Yarn Weight System

Categories of yarn, gauge ranges, and recommended needle and hook sizes

Yarn Weight Symbol & Category Names	0 LACE	1 SUPER FINE	2 FINE	3 LIGHT	4 MEDIUM	5 BULKY	6 SUPER BULKY	7 JUMBO
Type of Yarns in Category	Fingering, 10-Count Crochet Thread	Sock, Fingering, Baby	Sport, Baby	DK, Light Worsted	Worsted, Afghan, Aran	Chunky, Craft, Rug	Bulky, Roving	Jumbo, Roving
Knit Gauge Range in Stockinette Stitch to 4 inches*	33–40 sts**	27–32 sts	23–26 sts	21–24 st	16–20 sts	12–15 sts	7–11 sts	6 sts and fewer
Recommended Needle in Metric Size Range	1.5–2.25 mm	2.25–3.25 mm	3.25–3.75 mm	3.75–4.5 mm	4.5–5.5 mm	5.5–8 mm	8–12.75 mm	12.75 mm and larger
Recommended Needle in U.S. Size Range	000 to 1	1 to 3	3 to 5	5 to 7	7 to 9	9 to 11	11 to 17	17 and larger
Crochet Gauge Ranges in Single Crochet to 4 inches*	32–42 double crochets**	21–32 sts	16–20 sts	12–17 sts	11–14 sts	8–11 sts	7–9 sts	6 sts and fewer
Recommended Hook in Metric Size Range	Steel*** 1.6–1.4 mm Regular hook 2.25 mm	2.25–3.5 mm	3.5–4.5 mm	4.5–5.5 mm	5.5–6.5 mm	6.5–9 mm	9–15 mm	15 mm and larger
Recommended Hook in U.S. Size Range	Steel 6, 7, 8*** Regular hook B–1	B–1 to E–4	E–4 to 7	7 to I–9	I–9 to K–10½	K–10½ to M–13	M–13 to Q	Q and larger

* GUIDELINES ONLY: The above reflect the most commonly used gauges and needle or hook sizes for specific yarn categories.
** Lace weight yarns are usually knitted or crocheted on larger needles and hooks to create lacy, openwork patterns.
   Accordingly, a gauge range is difficult to determine. Always follow the gauge stated in your pattern.
*** Steel crochet hooks are sized differently from regular hooks—the higher the number, the smaller the hook, which is the reverse of regular hook sizing.

Source: Craft Yarn Council of America's **www.YarnStandards.com**

NOTES ON THE INSTRUCTIONS

- When a number appears before the stitch name, such as 3dc, work these stitches into the same stitch, for example "3dc into the next st."
- When only one stitch is to be worked into each of a number of stitches, it can be written like this, for example, "1sc in each of next 3 sts." When a number appears after a chain, for example, "ch 10," this means work the number of chains indicated.
- The asterisks mark a specific set of instructions that are repeated, for example, "* 2sc in next st, 1 dc in next st; rep from * across" means repeat the stitches from the first asterisk to next given instruction.
- When instructions are given with parentheses, they can mean three things. For example, "(2dc, ch 1, 2dc) in the next st" means work 2dc, ch 1, 2dc all into the same stitch. They can also mean a set of stitches repeated a number of times, for example, "(sc in next st, 2sc in next st) 6 times." Lastly, number(s) given at the end of row or round in the parentheses denote(s) the number of stitches or spaces you should have on that row or round.
- Be sure to read the Special Stitch(es) and Pattern Note(s) sections before beginning a project. You'll find new stitches and helpful hints there, and reading these notes will often clear up any questions about the project.

ABBREVIATIONS

beg	begin/begins/beginning
BLO	back loop only
bpdc	back post double crochet
ch(s)	chain/chains
ch-	refers to chain or space previously made
ch sp(s)	chain spaces(s)
cm	centimeters
dc	double crochet
dc2tog	double crochet 2 stitches together
FLO	front loop only
fpdc	front post double crochet
g	grams
hdc	half double crochet
hdc2tog	half double crochet 2 stitches together
in	inches
lp(s)	loop(s)
mm	millimeter
oz	ounces
rem	remaining
rep(s)	repeat(s)
rnd(s)	round(s)
RS	right side
sc	single crochet
sc2tog	single crochet 2 stitches together
sk	skip
sl st(s)	slip stitch(es)
sp(s)	space(s)
st(s)	stitch(es)
tog	together
tr	treble
WS	wrong side
yd(s)	yards

HOW TO HOLD YOUR HOOK

There are different ways that you can hold your hook, but I want to show you two of the most common. Try both and use the one that feels most comfortable.

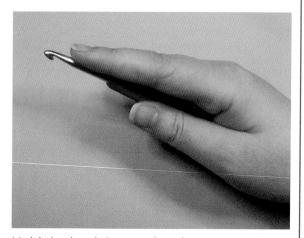

KNIFE HOLD

Hold the hook in your hand as you would a knife. Your hand is over the hook, using your thumb and middle finger to control hook while the pointer finger is on top guiding the yarn.

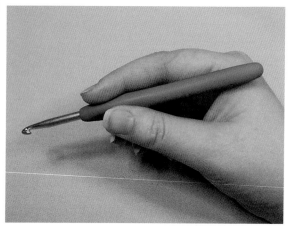

PENCIL HOLD

Hold the hook as you would a pencil. The hook is cradled in your hand resting on your middle finger.

STITCH GUIDE

This adjustable knot will begin every crochet project.

Step 1: Make a loop in the yarn.

Step 3: Pull tight on the yarn and adjust to create the first loop.

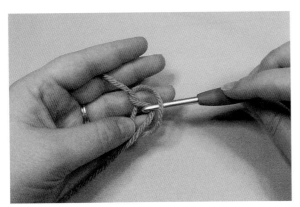

Step 2: With your crochet hook or finger, grab the yarn from the skein and pull through loop.

MAGIC RING

Many pieces worked in rounds will start with a magic ring.

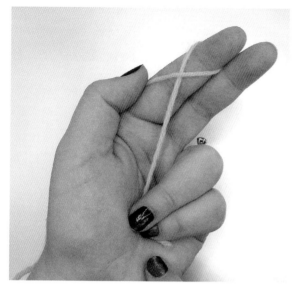

Step 1: Hold end of yarn with pinky and ring finger, wrap yarn around pointer finger as shown.

Step 2: Insert hook through loop on pointer finger and pull up loop.

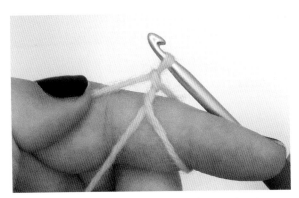

Step 3: Chain one. This is an important step.

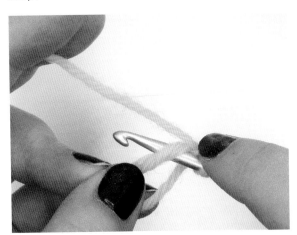

Step 4: Follow pattern and crochet into the loop and OVER the tail at the same time.

Step 5: When you have completed pattern directions, pull the beginning yarn tail until the center opening is tight and closed. Knot on wrong side to hold in place securely.

CHAIN (CH)

The chain provides the foundation for your stitches at the beginning of a pattern. It can also serve as a stitch within a pattern and can be used to create an open effect.

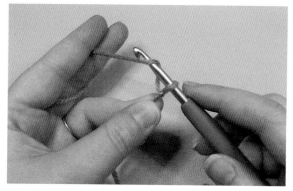

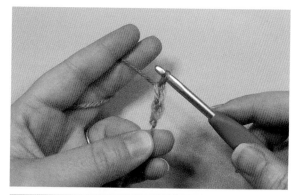

Step 1: Insert hook through the slipknot and place the yarn over the hook by passing the hook in front of the yarn.

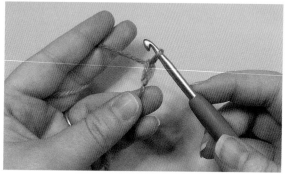

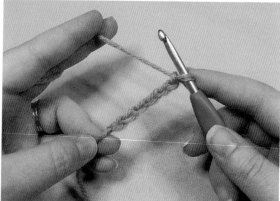

Step 3: Repeat Steps 1 and 2 to create multiple chains.

Step 2: Keeping the yarn taught (but not too tight) pull the hook back through the loop with the yarn. Ch 1 is complete.

SINGLE CROCHET (SC)

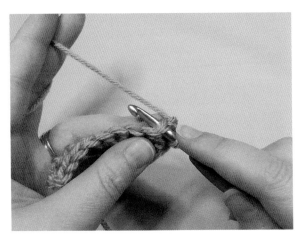

Step 1: Insert hook from the front of the stitch to the back and yarn over.

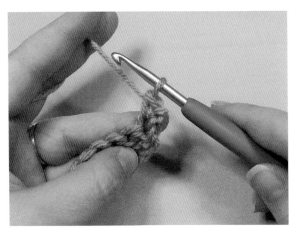

Step 3: Yarn over and draw through both loops on the hook to complete.

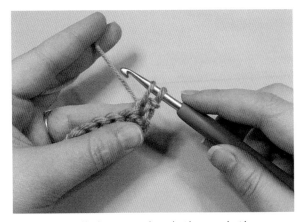

Step 2: Pull the yarn back through the stitch: 2 loops on hook.

WORKING INTO A STITCH

Unless specified otherwise, you will insert your hook under both loops to crochet any stitch.

WORKING INTO FRONT LOOP OR BACK LOOP

At times you will be instructed to work in the front loop only (FLO) or the back loop only (BLO) of a stitch to create a texture within the pattern.

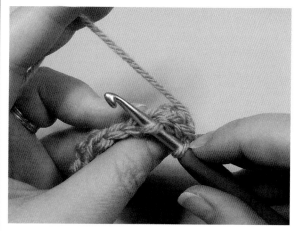

Insert hook to crochet into the front loop only (FLO) of a stitch.

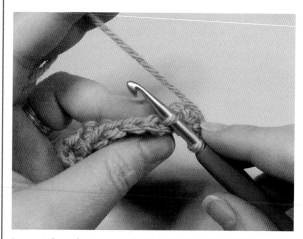

Insert hook to crochet into the back loop only (BLO) of a stitch.

SLIP STITCH (SL ST)

The slip stitch is used to join one stitch to another, or to join a stitch to another point. It can also be used within the pattern as a stitch without height.

Step 1: Insert the hook from the front of the stitch to the back of stitch and yarn over.

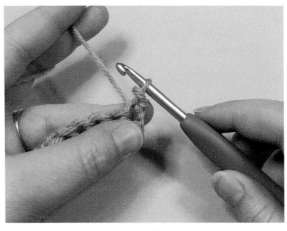

Step 3: Continue to pull the loop through the first loop on the hook to finish.

Step 2: Pull the yarn back through the stitch: 2 loops on hook.

HALF DOUBLE CROCHET (HDC)

Step 1: Yarn over.

Step 3: Yarn over and pull yarn back through stitch: 3 loops on hook.

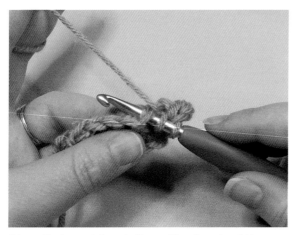

Step 2: Insert hook from the front of the stitch to the back.

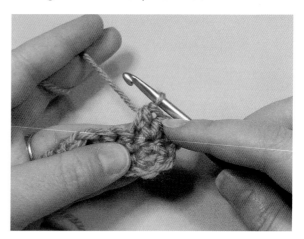

Step 4: Yarn over and draw through all 3 loops on hook to complete.

WORKING IN THE HALF DOUBLE CROCHET "3RD LOOP"

Step 1: Locate the top loops you normally work into.

Step 3: Work into the hdc 3rd loop as you would a regular stitch.

Step 2: On the WS (or back side) of the hdc, you'll see a horizontal bar. This is the 3rd loop of the hdc.

DOUBLE CROCHET (DC)

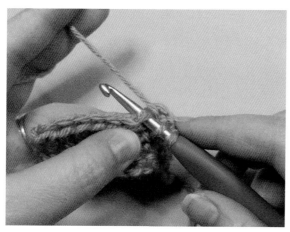

Step 1: Yarn over and insert the hook from the front of the stitch to the back.

Step 2: Yarn over and pull the yarn back through the stitch: 3 loops on hook.

Step 3: Yarn over and draw the yarn through the first 2 loops on the hook: 2 loops on hook.

Step 4: Yarn over and draw the yarn through the last 2 loops on hook to complete.

TREBLE CROCHET (TR)

Step 1: Yarn over 2 times.

Step 2: Insert the hook from the front of the stitch to the back. Yarn over and pull the yarn back through the stitch: 4 loops on hook.

Step 3: To complete: (Yarn over and draw the yarn through the first 2 loops on the hook) 3 times.

SINGLE CROCHET 2 TOGETHER (SC2TOG)

A single crochet 2 together (also known as a decrease) will take two stitches and make them into one single crochet stitch.

Step 1: Insert the hook from the front of the stitch to the back and yarn over. Pull the yarn back through the stitch: 2 loops on hook.

Step 3: Yarn over and draw through all 3 loops on the hook to complete.

Step 2: Leaving the loops on the hook, insert the hook front to back in the next stitch. Yarn over and pull back through stitch: 3 loops on hook.

INVISIBLE SINGLE CROCHET 2 TOGETHER

You may use the invisible single crochet 2 together for any sc2tog to create a less visible decrease:

Step 1: Insert hook in the FLO of next 2 stitches and yarn over.

Step 2: Draw through both stitches, yarn over and draw through 2 loops on hook (counts as one sc).

DOUBLE CROCHET 2 TOGETHER (DC2TOG)

A double crochet 2 together will take 2 stitches and make them into one double crochet stitch.

Step 1: Yarn over and insert the hook from the front of the stitch to the back. Yarn over and pull the yarn back through the stitch: 3 loops on hook.

Step 3: Leaving the loops on the hook, yarn over, insert the hook from front to back into the next stitch. Yarn over and pull back through the stitch: 4 loops on hook.

Step 2: Yarn over and draw the yarn through the first 2 loops on the hook: 2 loops on hook.

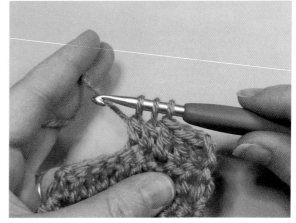

Step 4: Yarn over and draw the yarn through the first 2 loops on the hook: 3 loops on hook.

Step 5: Yarn over and draw the yarn through all 3 loops on hook to complete.

WORKING ON THE POST OF THE STITCH

Each stitch has a post. When working a front post stitch or back post stitch, use the post instead of the top stitch. This is the double crochet post.

FRONT POST DOUBLE CROCHET (FPDC)

Step 1: Yarn over, insert the hook from the front to the back to the front around the post of the stitch.

Step 2: Yarn over and pull the yarn back around the post: 3 loops on the hook.

Step 3: Complete like a double crochet: Yarn over and draw the yarn through the first 2 loops on the hook: 2 loops on the hook. Yarn over and draw the yarn through the last 2 loops on the hook to complete.

BACK POST DOUBLE CROCHET (BPDC)

Step 1: Yarn over, insert the hook from back to front to back around the post.

Step 3: Complete like a double crochet: Yarn over and draw the yarn through the first 2 loops on the hook: 2 loops on the hook. Yarn over and draw the yarn through the last 2 loops on the hook to complete.

Step 2: Yarn over and pull the yarn back around the post: 3 loops on the hook.

COLOR CHANGE

When changing colors, use this technique:

Step 1: Complete your given stitch until the last pull through.

Step 3: Continue working with joined color.

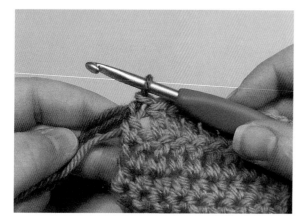

Step 2: Yarn over with the new color and pull through to finish the stitch and color change. Cut or drop the yarn from the original color.

INVISIBLE JOIN

Step 1: Complete your last stitch, cut yarn leaving a long end and pull yarn all the way through last stitch/loop.

Step 2: Thread yarn needle with long end, skip 1 stitch, insert yarn needle from front to back of next stitch.

Step 3: Skip the skipped stitch, insert yarn needle into the last stitch in the back loop from left to right (photo shows which back loop to use, but not in the direction; insert left to right).

Step 4: Pull yarn loosely to create a new loop over the skipped loop. Photo shows how the invisible join creates a "loop" to finish the work. Weave in the ends on wrong side of work.

ACKNOWLEDGMENTS

To my awesome husband, thank you for your continued support. You are amazing, and I love you so much! Our family and adventures inspire me to design and crochet all the goodies! To my testers, thanks so much for every little edit! And to the staff, I appreciate everything you do to make this book what it is!